THE **WEIGHT** *of* BEAUTIFUL

THE **WEIGHT** *of*
BEAUTIFUL

JACKIE GOLDSCHNEIDER

GALLERY BOOKS
New York   London   Toronto   Sydney   New Delhi

G

Gallery Books
An Imprint of Simon & Schuster, Inc.
1230 Avenue of the Americas
New York, NY 10020

First Gallery Books hardcover edition September 2023

GALLERY BOOKS and colophon are registered trademarks of Simon & Schuster, Inc.

For information about special discounts for bulk purchases, please contact Simon & Schuster Special Sales at 1-866-506-1949 or business@simonandschuster.com.

The Simon & Schuster Speakers Bureau can bring authors to your live event. For more information or to book an event, contact the Simon & Schuster Speakers Bureau at 1-866-248-3049 or visit our website at www.simonspeakers.com.

Interior design by Jaime Putorti

Manufactured in the United States of America

10 9 8 7 6 5 4 3 2 1

Library of Congress Cataloging-in-Publication Data has been applied for.

ISBN 978-1-6680-2380-8
ISBN 978-1-6680-2382-2 (ebook)

To anyone struggling in silence, you are not alone.

CONTENTS

CONTENTS

THE **WEIGHT** *of*
BEAUTIFUL

INTRODUCTION

꒰꒱

If you want to keep a secret, you must also hide it from yourself.

—George Orwell, *1984*

saw goosebumps all over my rawboned arm as I reached out to help Evan slice our wedding cake. I'd known there'd be air-conditioning at my August wedding, but I was excruciatingly cold, so I tensed the sides of my back together hard toward the center, trying to subtly move my body and warm myself up. It didn't work, but I couldn't complain about it in the middle of my reception. Besides, nobody else seemed cold.

We had a beautiful cake, four layers high with ornate white buttercream, adorned with dark pink roses on each layer and a flood of light pink roses at the base. I couldn't have cared less—I wanted no part of that thing. I stared at the cake and thought of our tasting appointment a few months before, and the pâtissier who couldn't understand why I wouldn't taste anything. "I'm not a cake person," I'd said, to her confusion and insult. She'd crinkled her eyebrows and said that if I tried *her* cake, I'd be a cake person. I hated when people pushed me. It made my joints tighten and my head swim with angry responses. I wanted to leave, but instead I looked down and told her I hated cake and icing made me nauseated. No one wants a sick customer in their little French bakery, especially an elegant joint like this one on Manhattan's Upper West Side, so she focused her attention on my husband-to-be, who smiled widely and made her feel like he valued her skills, unlike his miserable fiancée. As she spoiled him with samples of different butter-creams and ganaches, they laughed about how hard it was to choose and how delicious everything was. I wasn't jealous, though, because food brought me no enjoyment, only pain. It didn't matter if I liked the samples or not because I had no intention of eating the final product.

I thought that maybe by the time I got to my actual wedding day, I might be a little less sick and a little more able to eat some cake, but I was in even worse shape at my wedding than I was six months earlier. I was desperate to get this ceremonial slicing over with. Cutting the cake in front of everyone wasn't a problem. Having it publicly fed to me certainly was.

I stood there shivering while the band played a sugary song in the background: Marvin Gaye's "How Sweet It Is (To Be Loved by You)." *Maybe it won't be so sweet to be loved by me,* I thought. *Maybe it'll actually be miserable to be loved by a woman who can't eat a bite of cake without losing her shit. Did he know how messed up I was and not care, or is he just scared to say anything?* I was ecstatic to finally marry Evan, but I was freezing and anxious and didn't want to deal with this cake, much less in front of our families and friends.

I looked away to avoid eye contact with the crowd of guests watching me, waiting to see if I would eat. I knew that's what they were doing, at least some of them. I bet more than a few of our guests were whispering about my body, about my spine protruding from my back, or asking their tablemates if I had a disease. *So I'll eat the cake*, I thought, *to prove them wrong—and because I have no choice—but I'll have to count it into my daily calories. I only have a few hundred calories allotted for tonight, and I want a glass of champagne later, but I'll have to overcount the cake to be safe. If my bite is too big, I'll need to skip the champagne, so it's important that I eat as little of it as possible. I'll count it as 80 calories or 100 calories, because it can't be more than a tablespoon, so maybe I'll say 120 calories just in case.*

Numbers were speeding through my head. *How much halibut did I eat before this?*

I should have been thinking about anything else at that exact moment, in the middle of the dance floor, in my delicate lace dress that hugged my chest, showing off every rib around my breastbone and the razor-sharp clavicles jutting out beneath my shoulders, but here I was, with my new husband ready to feed me the first bite of something I wouldn't eat again for almost fifteen years. I took that bite, strategically leaving as much on my lips as possible, making sure the icing stayed outside of my mouth so I could quickly wipe it off with a napkin and save myself some grief. Every calorie counts, every single last one of them, no matter when or where, even if it's your wedding day. But I did it, half a bite, and now I was done. *No more food tonight.*

From my mid-twenties forward, I spent my days hungry—starving, actually—and light-headed from a lack of food. My mind reeled with numbers and calculations, in a state of constant hyperawareness of calories in and calories out, a life focused on staying as thin as possible, incessantly terrified I'd be forced to miss a workout or be pushed to try someone's food. I knew other people didn't live like this. I wanted that kind of life, one in which *I* could stop living like this. I wanted to eat food and then stop when I was full and not spend the day worrying about it. I wanted to feel steady on my feet instead of feeling like I could faint at any moment. I wanted to skip a workout when I was sick and sit on the couch with a snack, then go back when I felt better.

I'd always plan to start eating again once major life events had passed, like my wedding or having children. But then I'd come up with a story to tell myself and build in excuses so that I'd never have to follow through. The excuses went something like this: *I'll get married, and then I'll start eating once the wedding is over, because I already altered my dress so small that I can't take it out. But I should wait a few months after the wedding to start eating, because then everyone will say I got fat and let myself go once I locked in a husband, so I'll just wait until I get pregnant. Once I get pregnant, I'll have no choice but to eat more for the baby, and by the time I give birth, people will be used to me being bigger and it won't be so jarring. But I'm entitled to lose some of the baby weight, and I'll be miserable if I don't, so I'll wait until I'm done having kids, and then I'll reset everything with a strong mom-body. I'll start strength training and do fun workouts with my friends instead of just sprinting an hour a day. But I'll lose all the baby weight first and then start fresh.*

Then months became years. Years became decades.

On a sunny afternoon in 2019, I tried to seem relaxed as I sat down to lunch with my castmates, out on the wooden deck of a friendly Mexican restaurant in Westhampton Beach, New

York. The microphone's transmitter box knocked against my spine every time I leaned back in my chair, but even with the discomfort, I felt pretty good about this meal, compared to most meals, where I'd have to frantically scan the menu for something—anything—I could safely eat without worrying that it had so many calories I might've just destroyed my diet and my body. I'd been to this restaurant before with my family, when we came to our beach house where I was hosting the other Housewives, so I knew what to order. In fact, I had planned my order in my head before I even woke up that morning.

Cast trips were the hardest parts of every season because there were so many meals to manage and so many excuses to make, and I couldn't just go home and not eat in private. I had two jobs on cast trips: the first was to film a reality show, and the second was to eat enough to make sure no one thought I had a problem, without eating so much that my life would fall apart. The latter job was unquestionably harder.

Before these trips, I always made a plan with a detailed schedule of calories rationed throughout the day, excuses to avoid unsafe foods, foods I could eat in a multitude of situations, and a strategy to compensate for any missed cardio sessions. The rules were all written down in my food diary, so I could go back at any point to check that I'd made no mistakes with anything I ate that day. And it was working, I thought. Two years into being a Housewife, and no one had noticed I was sick. No one had noticed I was torturing myself every minute of every day or that I was famished while I moved the food on my plate to get to the lettuce. No one had noticed I was anorexic.

And then they did.

"Margaret said you have issues with food," Jennifer, one of my castmates, suddenly announced to the table, and I wondered if my world was about to crumble.

Maybe this was my chance to confess everything. For a split second, I considered it. The same way that, when you're driving over a bridge, you think for a split second about what might happen if you veer hard to the right. The world would end, at least as you know it, so of course you'd never do it. But for a second, you let yourself wonder about it. It was the first time since I had started all of this toxic shit—since my doctor had encouraged my first starvation diet when I was seventeen and I was desperate to be anything other than the heavy, invisible girl in the halls of my high school—that anyone who actually knew me had called me out on my behavior around food. It was the first time in years that I was being questioned as to whether I was sick. And it was taking place on national television.

I could've come clean, but I wasn't ready to let go of anorexia. I hated it deeply, I hated the pain and the endless thoughts and the hold it had on everything in my life, but I also needed it. Anorexia was the only thing that gave me control when everything else felt out of my control, and it was the only thing that let me run so far away from the person I used to be that I was no longer recognizable. I traded everything—my health, my sanity, my ability to socialize without anxiety—to hold on to my eating disorder. I gave it everything, and in return, it let the old me disappear.

I lived a life dominated by starvation, where no one dared to ask me if I needed help. For almost two decades, my diet followed a strict set of rules that were never stretched or broken, bound to maintaining a dangerously low body weight. There was no flexibility, there were no days off from exercise, there were no indulgences. And for all that time, through dating and marriage, infertility, parenting, and eventual fame, it was all done in secret.

And now here I was, living in hiding while in front of the cameras on one of the world's most popular reality shows, facing millions of people every week who somehow, without really knowing me, came to know my truth. I could no longer hide my brutal struggle with an eating disorder—a struggle that impacts thirty million Americans, fueled by diet culture, social media, and the dangerous promise of perfection.

This is my story, but it is also the story of millions of people like me, suffering in silence and striving to lead healthy, happy lives in recovery from eating disorders. My story is for all of us.

CHAPTER ONE

୨୦

WHAT LIES BENEATH US

All I ever wanted was to be thin. But wishing for it did nothing, so *thin* eluded me throughout my adolescence. As a teenager, I'd stare at my reflection and use my right pointer finger to pull the soft, puffy skin under my chin toward my neck, stretching it smooth and taut, as I sucked my cheekbones in all the way to see how my face would look if it were thin. I'd twist my head around in the mirror, checking all the angles of my glamorous new profile, feeling momentarily pretty, until I had to let it go. I didn't know how to make that face stay instead of mine.

I wasn't *obsessed* with losing weight when I was little—not the way I obsessed about it as a teen. As a young kid, I wasn't skinny or heavy, just somewhere in the middle: a little stocky with a cute puff of belly, and it didn't bother me much. Sometimes I'd look at my body's reflection and imagine being leaner, like a model. I'd suck in my tummy as much as I could, arching my back to stretch out my solid frame, examining my suddenly visible ribs with delight. But then I'd exhale and move on with my day without thinking about it again.

What really bothered me as a little kid in the eighties was having hair like a boy. My mom kept my brown hair cut so short I couldn't do anything but brush it and watch the little hairs on the sides feather out like a wet pigeon. Forget the body—what eight-year-old me *really* wanted was long blonde hair. *That's what'll make me pretty*, I thought, having hair like Daryl Hannah in *Splash,* or like all the perfect Barbies in my closet. But since my puffy dark coif grew sideways instead of down, that wasn't happening, either, so I didn't waste much time letting it upset me. I liked myself back then. I loved my friends, and I loved my block on Staten Island, where all the neighborhood kids played manhunt in each other's backyards. I played outside all day, roller-skating up and down the smooth sidewalks along my street and riding my bike for hours without a parent in sight. In the summers, my brother, Eric, and I would fill enormous green plastic garbage cans with water in our driveway and climb inside, dunking up and down and up and down in our personal makeshift pools. Eric was my favorite playmate growing up. I always knew he was different, but I didn't realize he was disabled until I was about nine years old, when it hit me like a rock. I don't remember what he said or did on that specific day, but I remember watching the way he reacted to something, how he failed to understand the world around him, and I was struck by an overwhelming sadness. The day I realized that his life would never be the same as mine, and that his opportunities in life would never be the same as other people's opportunities, I lay in my bed and cried all night.

My childhood on Staten Island was beautiful but not fancy, my weekends spent with grandparents and cousins in Brooklyn, my days and night filled with friends and block parties. I loved school, I loved my neighbors, and I especially loved my best friend, Joanna, who lived right next door. Joanna and I had been inseparable ever since we had met in our strollers in 1979, when she was two years old and I was three. We wore matching outfits and celebrated each other's religious holidays. We stole her older brother's horror movies to watch with our fingers covering our eyes, and we drooled over his handsome Catholic-school friends. We never talked about our weight, never called ourselves ugly, never criticized our bodies, and never compared the size tags on our matching clothes, even though I'm sure hers were smaller than mine.

Everything changed in 1990, when I moved away just before I turned fourteen.

Toward the end of the eighties, my parents' businesses took off, especially my mother's tech business. She started a computer consulting firm in 1979 while she was working full-time as a consultant at Philip Morris. Once my parents started raking in the kind of f*ck-you money that American dreams are made of, they wanted a bigger house, away from Staten Island and its giant heaps of landfill. They wanted a big yard and a pool with a hot tub, and my mother wanted an easier commute than her long bus ride to and from Manhattan every day. So she moved her office headquarters to New Jersey, and my parents started building our brand-new house in a brand-new development—which was still 90 percent barren when we arrived. There were acres between the empty parcels, unfinished dirt paths, overgrown swaths of unkempt land lining the roads, and the nearest store was miles away.

On a spring day in early 1990, at thirteen years old, I sat alone on the steps of the development's model home, staring at the emptiness around me. As my parents spoke to the developers inside, I wondered what would happen to my life. *This can't happen, I don't want to leave everything I know.* It was too much to think about, but I had no say in the matter. *There's nobody here,* I remember thinking. *Who will be my friend?*

When I was little, it seemed like everyone in my house was trying to lose weight except me. My parents would diet, but they could never keep the weight off. There was always some bizarre new eating plan they were on, like a grapefruit diet or cottage cheese diet, or a weird new food on our kitchen counter that was supposed to increase your metabolism. We had strange exercise contraptions like ThighMasters and Jane Fonda tapes hanging around the living room. Even my sister, who's five years older than I am and with whom I have no relationship, seemed to starve herself to model-like proportions for local beauty pageants every year and then gain it all back when it was over. Our childhood as sisters was one aggression after another, until endless fighting as kids turned into endless hostility as adults, giving way to eventual estrangement. Sometimes I'm sad to have a living, breathing sister who's essentially a stranger, but estrangement feels like a much more peaceful option for my life. Despite the fact that we never got along, I always thought that my sister looked so beautiful when she was skinny.

My parents kept a stockpile of diet soda at our Staten Island home, in the corner of the kitchen next to the basement door. The soda came in tall glass bottles, in dozens of exciting flavors like orange and black cherry, all with the same giant label on top that read "Dietetic" and a warning underneath that said something like "This product contains ingredients that cause cancer in lab animals." I used to read the label over and over, my seven-year-old brain intrigued—I didn't know exactly what it meant but had a feeling it might not be good—and then I'd guzzle a bottle in its entirety.

My mother kept thick calorie guides stacked on our bookshelves, stuffed between her Stephen King novels and my dad's Ken Follett thrillers. When she wasn't doing a fad diet, she'd try to lose weight by counting calories. I didn't care about her books, not the Stephen Kings or the calorie guides. I didn't care if my mom was skinny or fat, if she wore fancy clothes or pretty makeup. I was just proud that she was the smartest mom of any mom I knew. None of my friends had a mom who owned a business in Manhattan like she did. "Jackie, when I was in high school, I used to stop at the newsstands in Brooklyn and look at pictures of girls in magazines," she'd later tell me. "There was one girl in a yellow bikini, and I'll never forget, she was so beautiful that I cried. I looked up at God and I said, 'I would trade every brain cell I have for a body like that,'" she said. "I hated that God made me smart instead of making me thin."

But God didn't just make her smart, he made her brilliant, and she worked like an animal with that God-given brain that she would've traded for that size-zero waist. "I hated being chubby in high school," my mother said. She wanted to be popular, and she wanted boys to like her, both of which—she believed—required her to be thin. "When I was chubby, I'd go to parties and I'd sit on the couch and read while all the other girls were having fun," she recalled. By the time she got pregnant at twenty-one years old, my happily married mother had all but given up on chasing beauty, save for the liquid eyeliner she'd wear to meet with clients. She spent all her time making money and none of her time trying to be glamorous. It took too much effort that she didn't want to make, and too much time and money that she didn't have to spend.

Unsurprisingly, I grew up knowing absolutely nothing about style, with a mother who couldn't have cared less about fashion. She loathed shopping, hated makeup, and demonized the type of women who wore high heels or painted their nails red, probably because she knew she could never be one of them. Those were the women who lived leisurely lives, shopping and lunching, while she worked day and night; who went to neighborhood parties that she wasn't invited to; and who left her out of everything, as she'd tell me. I never questioned why she hated people she hardly knew, or why she constantly seemed angry about their lives. Maybe these women reminded my mother of the girls who left her out when she was in high school. Maybe it was comforting to her to be the victim, and to believe that people didn't invite her because they were assholes and they liked nice things because they were shallow. I always felt bad when she seemed so angry at the world, but once I was a teen and could understand her feelings, I was already pretty sad about my own social standing. And since I couldn't do anything to make her feel better about other people, I just shut up and tried to get through the days.

For the entirety of my childhood and teenage years, my mother worked endlessly. Most weekdays, she'd walk into the house after dark, around eight p.m., exhausted by a double blow of work stress and guilt over missing out on her children's daily lives. On week-ends, she'd pacify that guilt by overfeeding us. She'd cook piles of food—thirty meatballs at a time, large vats of soups, stews, rice, fish, meats; she'd buy huge brown bags of bagels in every variety, along with spreads and lox and whitefish salad and everything else you could think of. Then she'd encourage me to eat all of it. There was no malice, no intention to make me fat or feel sick, there was only love, in the biggest way she could think to deliver it. She wanted to fill her family with love, to buy us the world and make sure we wanted for nothing. She couldn't give us her time, so she gave us food.

I didn't know better back then. I was too young to connect the dots between mom guilt, her underprivileged upbringing, and her subsequent need to feed her children to the edges of nausea. Later in life, I blamed my mother's overfeeding for setting me up for a lifetime of disordered eating. I blamed her for teaching me how to override my body's fullness cues, how to eat for comfort, and how to use food as a substitute for love. "I never wanted to hurt you, but I had no control over it, Jackie," she told me not so long ago. "You just have to understand where I came from." The roots of my mother's need to stuff her loved ones silly started long before I came along, long before even she came along. It started on a train to Rus-sia in 1939.

My bubbe—my mother's mom—had lost her parents to cancer by the time Hitler killed her brothers and sisters in war-torn Poland. In 1939, Bubbe ran, hiding in a forest until she could get on a train to Russia. Zeidi—my mother's dad—was also on the train, running from the Nazis while his parents met their death in Treblinka. He had some bread, and Bubbe, who'd been starving for days, asked for a piece. They became a couple, arriving in Russia and living together in a refugee camp in Siberia with the rest of the Jews who were escaping certain death.

But death found them anyway. "There was no food there, Jackie," my mother told me. "My parents would walk outside and see dead bodies in the street. Everyone was dying of starvation." Zeidi told the refugees to gather their valuables each week—jewelry, coins, anything they had—and he'd get on a train to different Russian villages every so often to trade the valuables for potatoes or turnips, any food he could find. "He did that for a while, and he saved people's lives," my mother said, "but the Russians found out and arrested him for black-marketing. He went to jail and was sentenced to death." Zeidi was still in a Russian jail cell when the war ended in 1945, and my bubbe went back to Poland. "People told her not to wait for him, that he was dead, but she waited. The Jewish community kept track of where everyone was," she said. After five years and forty-eight days in prison, Zeidi made his way back to Poland, to my bubbe, and in 1947, they left for Israel, where my mother was born in 1949.

"Here I was, growing up on these stories of having no food and how a piece of bread or a potato is life-changing," she said. "For survivors of World War II, and the second generation like me, we all grew up worshipping food." My mother told me how piss-poor Israel was back then and how little there was to eat. "So many Jews were coming to Israel those first few years, and the country was so new that there weren't many kibbutzim yet," she said, referring to Israel's communal settlements, traditionally based in agriculture, where the wealth and food from the farming were shared equally by the people who lived and worked there. "But you have to farm for a while to really produce enough output to feed everyone," she explained. While people were starting kibbutzim during that time, there were so many newcomers that there wasn't enough food in Israel until later years. "So there was food rationing—it was called tzenah," she said, explaining that the Israeli government would give them coupons to buy eggs and bread in limited amounts. "My parents were so lucky to have chickens and ducks in their backyard, and people would come to them for extra food, so we only knew food as a miracle, a gift from God." She paused. "And whenever there was any extra food, my mother overfed me. Whatever there was, as much as there was, she fed it to me. We never knew if we'd run out again." Later in life, when food was no longer scarce, her parents' mentality, and her mentality, stayed the same.

"Bubbe overfed me, and when I became a mother, I overfed you," she said. "It was so drilled into me, I'm still always afraid there might not be any more food."

But there was plenty of food in New Jersey, especially in my new home. There was so much food that it cluttered the countertops, spilled from the pantries, and covered every inch of our fridge and freezer shelves. There were no friends and no neighbors. There were no parents to greet me after school. There was no Joanna, no roller skates, no sidewalks on my street, and no one riding bikes. There was no happiness for me as a teenager in suburban New Jersey. But oh man, there was food.

CHAPTER TWO

WELCOME TO WEIGHT WATCHERS

When I was fifteen years old, about a year after we moved, my mother's cousin called me zaftig, a Yiddish word meaning plump and juicy. She was right: I was definitely zaftig, and I hated every fucking thing about it. "We're all a little zaftig in our family, Jackie," she said. "Voluptuous women are more beautiful, anyway."

But I didn't want to be *that kind of beautiful.* I didn't think I looked beautiful, and neither did anyone at my new high school.

I moved to New Jersey a few weeks into my freshman year and started school without knowing a single person there except for my brother, Eric. Eric and I had never gone to the same school before. On Staten Island, he'd always attended schools that had programs for learning-disabled children. But our new high school had a program like that, and since Eric had been held back in grade school, we came in as freshmen together, like twins. Me, with my round face and bad hair, and my disabled brother, whom I loved fiercely and just wanted everyone else to love as well. Most kids were kind to Eric—they smiled back when he said hello and gave him high fives when he asked for them. Some kids just ignored us both, and that was fine, too. But for a handful of kids, mostly boys with a few girls in the mix, Eric was the answer to whatever insecurity or inner hatred they harbored. They went out of their way to be cruel to my brother, and they broke my heart on a daily basis.

Most days I'd walk into the lunchroom to find Eric doing karate moves atop a lunch table as a group of kids clapped in time and cheered him on. Other days, the same scene would play out with Eric dancing in a hallway, surrounded by cheering students. Eric was sure that everyone was clapping with excitement, as if he were wowing them with his moves and destroying his competition in a dance-off, but I knew that wasn't what they were doing. I could see the tears of laughter running down their faces. I wanted to grab them by the fucking hair and smash their ugly faces with my textbook, but I knew I couldn't do that. As they reveled in the spectacle they made of Eric, I often wondered how they'd feel if they had to watch that happen to their own disabled brother. Kids made up fake names for Eric to call them, and other kids suddenly pulled their hand away when he went for a high five. For a cheap laugh, some people made him the messenger of stupid or perverted misinformation. He wanted so badly to please everyone that he'd graciously agree to relay what people sent him to say, for example, telling a girl "Joe said you were great last night" and crap like that. When everyone laughed, he thought he'd made them happy. Sometimes his lunch money was stolen, and occasionally, a kid would throw a pencil at his head to see his reaction. Eric never got that mad; he just got sad, and he'd forgive everyone on a dime.

But I got mad, really incredibly fucking mad. I was the stopper. Everything I saw, I had to stop, because I loved Eric fiercely, because I protected him instinctively, and because I was the only one who would bother to intervene. With pulsing embarrassment, gripped by anger and fear, I was forever pulling Eric out of crowds and down from tables, to a parade of booing. I hated being the stopper—I was already the ugly new kid, and now I was busting up everyone's good time. Every now and then, I hesitated to intervene and hated myself for wondering whether it would end on its own if I let it play out, because I wanted people to like me, too. Every day was hell, but the worst day came late in my freshman year.

One morning at school, a group of kids told Eric to take off his shoes, and then they flushed them down the toilet in the boys' bathroom. The shoes didn't go down, of course, just rumbled around in the toilet as the kids pumped the flusher, but they tried nonetheless. Eric spent the rest of the school day in socks. I was called to the guidance counselor's office, where I sat, numb, in a chair while she and the assistant principal relayed the story and assured me the kids who'd done it would be disciplined. In the nineties, shit like that got you a few days' suspension at the most. *Is that supposed to be enough for me? Is that supposed to be enough for my parents?* I got a burning sensation in the tip of my nose, and my heart felt like it weighed a thousand pounds. *Don't cry, Jackie. Not here.* I wanted these boys to feel the same pain that I felt upon hearing the story, the pain my parents felt when they found out that their handicapped son had to walk around school shoeless because these kids spat on our family and would now spend the rest of their week at home playing Nintendo. When I left the guidance counselor's office, I went into the girl's bathroom, knelt in a stall, and cried so hard I couldn't breathe. I was broken. I couldn't understand how anyone could be that cruel or set out to hurt someone so vulnerable. I still don't understand the viciousness of bullying, and Eric never understood it, either. I could handle people disliking me, but I never got used to them being mean to Eric. When Eric looks back on high school, he doesn't remember people being mean to him. I'm happy he doesn't.

I started gaining weight soon after I left Staten Island. Most days I got off the school bus, walked into an empty house, took out my homework in the kitchen, and riffled through the refrigerator for something, *anything,* that felt good going down. Leftovers, bags of cold cuts, or plastic containers of tuna salad from the deli—eating them felt good. These foods became companions to my loneliness, and momentarily filled an emptiness inside me. I denied myself of nothing, ate whatever I felt like eating, and that made me happy when little else in my new life could. Sometimes I'd raid the pantry, opening bags of chips or boxes of cereals, or I'd take bagels from the paper bag full that was always rolled up on the kitchen counter. As I arranged my homework into piles, I'd start eating. I had no neighborhood friends to meet outside to play with, no town to walk to, and with both parents at work, I had no rides anywhere. I'd snack through hours of homework, until dinnertime, when I usually ate alone or, occasionally, with Eric. My dad generally ate in front of the TV after work, watching whatever sports games he had bets on as he screamed at the screen, and my mother didn't get home until past eight. I'd eat alone through dinner, and snack more as I watched TV at night after dinner. I ate whatever was in the house, whatever the housekeeper cooked, and whatever was left sitting in the fridge. As I got bigger, my self-esteem plummeted.

I wish I could be like Eric and forget the way people treated me in high school. It wasn't that they were so mean all the time; it was more that they looked right through me, like if I disappeared, no one would even care or notice. I wish I could forget how worthless it made me feel, and how I envied the girls who were prettier, the ones who ran in tight circles of popular kids and always seemed so happy. I wish I could forget how badly I wanted to be one of them, especially the one I thought of as their queen bee. Her name was Stef.

The thought of Stef reminds me of how much I hated myself in high school. She was the embodiment of everything out of my reach: looks, popularity, body, happiness. Stef made me feel inadequate by doing absolutely nothing at all. She was every popular girl rolled into one. She was high school personified.

Stef was effortlessly pretty, the center of attention, and rail-thin—the opposite of zaftig. She had long full curls and a dusting of freckles on her nose. Everyone loved her, from the boys in varsity jackets who went by only their last names to the cliquey bad boys who had house parties and drank all of their parents' liquor. Stef wore white tank tops that showed off her shoulder blades and jeans that sloped down on her bony hips. She wore ChapStick and mascara instead of real makeup, not like the colors I drew on my face in the morning to try to be beautiful.

Stef always seemed to be floating through the hallways, laughing with her group of girlfriends. She must have smelled good also. She probably wore something trendy, like CK One, or maybe she smelled like lavender-scented deodorant, but I wouldn't know because I never got close enough to smell her. She wasn't my friend and probably didn't even know my name. When I was a sophomore, a classmate told me that boys wanted girls like Stef because they could pick them up with their pinkie.

That became my fifteen-year-old life goal. One day boys would want me because they could pick me up with their pinkie. But by junior year, I was as far from being that person as I could possibly be.

I wasn't delicate; I was big and rough-looking, with bushy hair and a soft, puffy face. I had rosacea on my cheeks, which made it look like I was always overheated. Most of my classmates looked right through me, and I couldn't blame them. I hated what I saw in myself, and I felt unworthy of attention. Every time a popular girl giggled with a friend, I dreamed of being her, and then I hated myself even more. I knew I had enough personality to win people over if they gave me a chance, but my body was destroying all my chances. If I were thin, I could be invited to house parties, and I could have boyfriends and laugh in the hallway and love my life, too. I would be beautiful one day if I were thin.

I had a few passing friendships at school, none that lasted longer than a year at a time, but the kids were much nicer at my New Jersey day camp, which I started attending the summer after my freshman year. I loved that day camp, relative to the rest of my life. I went back for four years. My camp friends were fun, they included me in their plans, and I knew they liked me, unlike my school friends, who were always fleeting. But I still always felt dispensable, like no one was ever looking for me or needed me to be there. I was never as cute as the other girls. In pictures, they were always posing with sexy smiles and good hair, and I was always the big girl on the side.

I could never wear cutoff shorts the way they did or knot my camp shirt into a crop top above my belly button without people laughing, and I hated that. But what made every bad feeling a thousand times worse was that I was absolutely boy-crazy.

In fact, I had a knack for finding an attractive feature in almost *any boy* that would make me fall head-over-heels infatuated with them. I'd been boy-crazy since as far back as I could remember. In kindergarten, I was obsessed with a boy named Jerome. At five years old, I told people he was my boyfriend and drew hearts around his picture in the kindergarten yearbook. Ever since then, I'd always had an unrequited crush on someone, often three or four boys at a time. I chose boys who never liked me back, even if no one else had a crush on them.

And only one thing ever gave me hope: slow songs about love.

Specifically, I was enamored with the corniest eighties ballads I could find. I would listen to them alone, eyes closed and head back, daydreaming about someone wanting me in return. I made mixtapes on which Journey and Air Supply would blubber in schmaltzy lyrics about heartache and loss, pining for someone to come back and promising to love them forever. *So here I am / With open arms / Hoping you'll see / What your love means to me.* The songs would stream full volume through my headphones as I lay down and imagined one of my crushes falling in love with me. *I'm all out of love, what am I without you? / I can't be too late to say that I was so wrong . . .* The songs wailed into my ears as I'd picture a boy kissing me during a slow dance, or maybe he'd pull me in for a romantic smooch as we walked to our bus through the camp parking lot, and for a moment, I'd be desirable. Except I was always thinner in my daydreams.

During my junior year in high school, I was dying for a boy-friend to take to my junior prom, or at least someone who might kiss me before the night ended, even if he never spoke to me again. Instead, I took my friend Dan from summer camp. Dan was sweet, he said yes as soon as I asked him to be my date, but he wasn't in-terested in me like that, and I was just grateful to have a date at all. People always said I had a pretty face, and I sort of believed that, so I thought that maybe I could find a way to make myself look beau-tiful on prom night. Turned out few things made me feel worse than prom-dress shopping.

First I tried the mall, though I hated the mall, where the girls in my grade shopped in little groups, parading around the dressing rooms to repeated chants of "Oh my God you look soooo good." The stores at the mall were for skinny girls, especially the worst store in the whole world, 5-7-9. All the popular girls got their cute little crappy clothes from 5-7-9, where everything in the store was either a size 5, a size 7, or a size 9. In today's sizing, it would probably be called 0-2-4, and I'm sure everyone would have a total fucking meltdown about it. But back then it was fine to let girls know that if you had normal-size thighs or a human-size ass, you weren't welcome to shop there. I couldn't fit my left foot into any of their clothes. 5-7-9 made me feel like an outcast, more than any other trendy store at the mall. More than Abercrombie & Fitch or Express or the Limited—at least those stores didn't have names that let me know I couldn't be inside as anything more than an observer. 5-7-9 made me feel so bad that I didn't want to go near it. So I didn't go near it, or most of the other stores in the mall, for that matter, except the ones that sold giant rock-band T-shirts or incense. I never even tried to wear anything cute.

I shopped alone, hoping to find a dress, walking store to store, trying to find something that would close or clasp, and finding nothing. I also tried boutiques and department stores, but I was too big for standard sizing. I wouldn't be caught dead in the plus-size corner of Nordstrom or the shopping-center stores with the larger sizes where some of the bigger moms in town shopped, but I couldn't yank the closure up on any dresses in the trendy places where my classmates were buying theirs. I stood in dressing rooms full of spaghetti-strapped options, where sequined and taffeta gowns hung on the wall in in the largest sizes I could find, as I stared in the mirror behind me at zippers that had acres of my back dividing them. I'd suck my stomach in as far as it could go, but it wouldn't make a dent.

I was too embarrassed to shop with any of the girls I was friendly with at school. I didn't want them to see me as more of an outcast or give them a reason to pity me. I didn't want to watch them buy things off the rack while I stood there pathetically empty-handed and waiting to leave. I could have shopped with my mom, but she worked so much. Besides, she would always try to soften a blow to my self-esteem by telling me that I was "the most gorgeous person" she'd ever seen in her whole entire life, and it pissed me off. Any time I got dressed in something that wasn't stretchy, my mom would feign complete awe and exclaim, "You look like you just stepped off the cover of *Vogue*." I liked it when I was little, but now it made me want to yell at her and call her a fucking liar. She finally offered to take me to a dressmaker to have something custom-made. It seemed like a good option, and no one had to know. But my mother knew absolutely nothing about clothing or fashion. She had come to America in the sixties from Israel as an impoverished immigrant, and from then on, she'd been completely uninterested in anything stylish. Despite her best intentions, I ended up with a crudely designed mass of black satin, fitted on top with spaghetti straps and an A-line bottom, and a piece of lace glue-gunned over my breasts. I looked and felt enormous. Pictures of me in that dress still hit me like a brick, with every feeling of sadness palpable.

My father insisted on filming me as I left the house for prom, and the more I implored him not to, the closer he brought the camera. My dad loved taking videos of his kids, particularly when we didn't want him to, and despite his good nature, he found it irresistibly funny when we begged him to stop filming. There are countless videos of me fighting with my sister, or self-consciously going into the pool, where I'm pleading to shut off the camera, ending with a close-up of my hand rapidly approaching to block the lens and my dad laughing hysterically.

Given my hatred of being filmed, it's astounding that I ended up with a career in front of a camera. But back then, and particularly on junior-prom day, I didn't want him recording me because I hated the way I looked. I hated myself and my dress. I hated the way the lady at the mall's unisex salon—with its cheesy wall of pictures of kids who looked like Pat Benatar and the stench of perm solution and Aqua Net—did my hair in spiral curls, and I hated knowing that my date, who was just a friend, wouldn't even hold my hand.

Even now, my dad will pull out that video just to show me how fat I was.

He finds the whole thing funny—hysterical, actually—and he thinks I should also. After all, I'm thin now, so why not have a good laugh about the whole damn thing? "Look how *big* you were," he'll say with a massive grin, pointing at the screen to a scene of me walking to Dan's car in my ugly black dress. "Can you believe that's your mommy?" he'll ask if my kids are there with me. He's not trying to be cruel, I'm sure of that, it's just that weight, in my father's mind, is only a *thing*. It's a thing you lose, in which case you celebrate; or a thing you gain, in which case you plan your next diet. He thinks gaining weight sucks, and all diets suck, and you do what you have to do to drop the pounds, and you don't cry about how hard it was, because every diet is hard, and it's as simple as that. And if you manage to lose a whole ton of weight, you should be so incredibly proud of yourself that you can laugh at the fat person you used to be, no matter how painful it was for you to be obese, no matter how much you tortured yourself to be thin. In my father's eyes, I beat the weight-loss game. I clobbered it. I was a champion at weight loss, so let's laugh about it together.

I don't get mad at my dad for laughing at how I looked, because he doesn't understand how it felt to be a teenage girl who hated herself, and he never will. I don't get mad at him for thinking I should be proud of how much weight I lost, because he has absolutely no comprehension of what an eating disorder truly is, how devastating it is, and all the ways it can kill you.

One time, during my second season on the show, my father showed my youngest children, then ten years old, the video from my junior prom, pointing at the screen to see if they recognized their own mother. "Who's that big girl?" he asked with a smile as a sadness came over me. I was sad that we were here again, watching my dad laugh about how "big" I was, and sad that my daughter was witnessing it firsthand, watching a man disparage her mother's body. I worried she might internalize that moment, holding it inside her until a day she thought about her own weight and suddenly remembered that you get laughed at if you're not thin. But I could also see that it didn't come from a bad place or an attempt to hurt me—he was just proud of how far I'd come from my teenage years. I tried to explain to my father how much dieting had cost me, but he couldn't wrap his head around the idea that losing weight could cause so much distress. "You're a good inspiration to kids who are heavy," he said, before telling me that battling an eating disorder was almost worth it. I knew how bad that would look when the show aired. *Stop, Dad, please stop, I can't explain this to you right now, I don't want to talk about this on camera.* My instinct was to protect my father, but he thought he was praising me, and he kept going. "Look at you now," he said, and I knew right then he had no idea the depths that I had gone to get to where I was. He couldn't hear what I was telling him, because the concept of an eating disorder was and is so foreign to him. I'm disappointed when he laughs, because it minimizes a lifetime of pain, and I know there's a deep, anguished part of me that he'll never understand. But maybe he can't understand what an eating disorder really is. Maybe he doesn't want to understand. He doesn't want to think about the bad stuff. He just wants to be proud of me.

B y the time I was a senior, I was obese. I was the girl who always watched and was never noticed, the one who thought everyone *else* was special and happy. I was the girl who had a crush on everyone and then watched them kiss everyone else. I wore loose boxers, men's jeans, and massive wool sweaters from Eddie Bauer. My favorite top was a navy blue merino wool Eddie Bauer sweater, in a men's XXL, that fell so loose around my torso that you couldn't tell what kind of body was underneath. I'd cuff the sleeves under my hands and hide in its volume. Those kinds of men's stretchy clothes were safe. I didn't have to tug them past my thighs until my fingertips took on the color of the fabric, or worry about getting my arm stuck in the opening of a sleeve. I had gotten used to being me, even if I didn't like who I was. But one day during my senior year, I was putting on lipstick in the hallway by my locker, and a boy named Nick walked by. He glanced slightly at me as he passed, and under his breath he said, "Don't bother, it won't help." He kept walking like he hadn't just taken all the air from my lungs.

What Nick said was the sentiment I recognized from most people, even if they never said it to me the way he did. His words hung there. *Don't bother, it won't help.* That day crushed me, and his words have never left me.

I never felt a connection to my New Jersey town, and from the moment I got there, I started thinking about going away to college. I'd dream about graduating and leaving everything about that town behind me. But the older and heavier I got, the more my college dreams changed. When I was a kid, I watched movies like *Revenge of the Nerds* and fantasized about being a sorority girl with a cute boyfriend at a rah-rah university, but I didn't want that anymore. By the time I took my SATs, I wanted to disappear into a big city where I didn't have to be friends with just the people behind the school gates. Anyway, I thought I was too fat for a campus school where everyone looked cute in their oversize sweatshirts. I didn't look cute in oversize sweatshirts; I just looked oversized. I dreaded having four more years of watching people forget about me and being rejected by the cool kids. I needed a place where I could walk a few blocks and be among families living normal lives, where I could be any size I happened to be, and be anonymous, and just worry about my future. In March 1994, I accepted a spot in the incoming fall freshman class at Boston University, ready to immerse myself in school and lose myself in a big city.

And then a weekday in April 1994 was the day my life changed.

I had an appointment with my family physician for a routine college physical. Any appointment about my body made me apprehensive. No one had to tell me I wasn't perfect; I was already aware of that. The nurse came in first and told me to get on the scale.

"I know what I weigh," I said with requisite teenage angst. "I'll just tell you what I weigh." She wrote down the number I gave her, took my blood pressure, and left the room. Crisis averted—I could breathe again.

The doctor walked in and told me he needed an accurate weight. I hated scales, especially random scales belonging to other people, especially scales belonging to men who wanted to judge my body. I didn't give a shit if he was a doctor, I didn't want him to weigh me. I gave him the same spiel I'd given the nurse, but he wasn't buying it.

"Jackie, I'll tell you what," he said, sighing. "Face backward, tell me what you really think you weigh, and if you're within ten pounds, I won't make you look."

I was too nervous to argue with him, so I agreed, picking a high enough number that I'd save myself the embarrassment of a lecture.

Maybe he'd even tell me I weighed less than I thought, and we could just high-five, finish, and say goodbye, and I could get the fuck out of his office. I stepped backward on the scale, squeezing my eyes shut as I listened to the counterweights behind my neck sliding all the way across the steel beam and then banging around for more weight.

I was off—*way* off—and well over two hundred pounds. My doctor told me to turn around, and with pulsing embarrassment, I looked at the scale. *Everything* about that moment—the way he took a deep breath and aggressively crossed out the number I had given the nurse, the way he quickly moved the counterweights back to zero so he could start his lecture—was telling me to be ashamed.

"You don't want to go to college fat," he said. I was mortified. It was the tone of voice that someone's teacher would use if a promising student was failing out, or if your kind uncle found your stash of drugs. He stared at me with disappointment, as though I were destroying my life at the tender age of seventeen and the only thing that could stop me was the palpable disgust in his voice. Plenty of people had called me fat over the previous few years, most behind my back and some to my face. But this was the first time someone had told me that I *needed* to change, that I shouldn't stay fat, and implied that I'd be an outcast forever in a bigger body. The fact that he was a medical expert made it feel even worse, like his words carried more sway than if anyone else had said them to me. I don't remember if he mentioned the supposed health benefits of losing weight, but he probably did, since he was a doctor. He probably talked about blood pressure and comorbidities for a minute, but I was too overcome by shame to pay attention to any of that. What I know for sure is that he emphasized the social benefits very clearly.

"You'll have more fun if you lose weight," he said. "Trust me."

I trusted him; of course I *fucking* trusted him. He was telling me shit I already knew, something I dreamed about and cried about, and I FUCKING KNEW IT BEFORE HE SAID IT. I was suddenly desperate to change my horrible body. I was suddenly desperate to lose weight.

"I don't know how," I told him.

But *he* knew how: Weight Watchers.

He said the receptionist had a Yellow Pages and would get me the number. He said to call them and see where they had local meetings, and they would help me lose weight. The receptionist gave me the number. I left the office, drove to the first pay phone I could find, and called Weight Watchers. They had a center at the local mall, and a meeting starting in an hour.

"Can you make it here in time?" the woman on the phone asked.

Fuck yeah, I could.

The lady at the front desk was nice and seemed genuinely happy to welcome me. I told her my name. "Welcome, Jackie!" she said. "Congratulations on taking the first step." I looked around at the piles of handouts stacked behind her chair as we waited for the group leader to come over. She had me fill out paperwork and told me it was time to weigh in.

The group leader brought me to a scale in plain view of everyone in the room. That day had been all about scales. It had begun with my doctor's steel medical scale. That scale sent me running from his office all the way to the mall, and now here, to this new white plastic scale, where I could finally do something about the mess that I'd created. One scale measured how much I had failed, but this one would measure how much I could accomplish. I would have preferred to be weighed privately, but I had no choice, so fuck it. I already felt like a total disaster. I already knew I was overweight; in fact, almost everyone there was some degree of fat except the group leader, who would be running the meeting. She wasn't really thin, more like average. *I'd kill to be average,* I thought.

She wrote my weight in the top space of a weekly check-in book and then gave me a packet of materials telling me what I could eat that week until my next weigh-in. I sat down on a beige folding chair, in a small room with a pebbled ceiling, among a dozen women ranging from chubby to obese, and flipped through the pages of their introductory pamphlet. And there they were: instructions for exactly what to do to get skinny. *Are you fucking kidding me?* I had been searching for this my whole life, the exact formula for being thin, and now I had it in my hands. I was a whiz at following directions; *I could do this.* But I wouldn't just do this, I would do it better than anyone else in the room. *I would kill it.*

As I listened to the group leader talk about calories and veggies, and which diet desserts we should try making this week, and how many minutes we should walk to work off a plum, I felt like I had found God. She told us how empowering it is to take control of your eating habits, and I could feel it in my soul. She told us how good it feels to know exactly what you're putting into your body, and I soaked up every word of it.

In the late eighties and early nineties, Weight Watchers used a program called Quick Start, which looked and felt to me like a starvation diet that made eating a game of exchanges (small servings) and options, so you could eat within extremely limited parameters and pray you weren't dying of hunger when you depleted your allowances. You could have certain vegetables, like cucumbers and lettuce, if you were hungry after your options ran out, and a few "free" calories a week to play with. Each day went something like this:

- 5 to 6 protein (meat) exchanges
- 2 milk exchanges
- 3 bread exchanges
- 3 fat exchanges
- 3 or more vegetable exchanges
- 1 optional exchange starting week 5
- Optional calories per week: 150 maximum week 1; 200 maximum week 2; 300 maximum week 3; 400 maximum week 4; 500 maximum week 5 and beyond.

It generally came out to under 1,000 calories per day, far less than an average body needs just to keep the organs working and carry out basic autonomic functions like breathing, digestion, and maintaining body temperature. It was certainly far less than my teenage body needed for fuel and nutrients. But I didn't know from any of that, and frankly, I didn't care. Weight Watchers was a massive business, and some of my parents' friends swore by it, so I trusted it, and by extension I trusted Quick Start. The extra 150 calories divided over 7 days came to 22 calories a day. That's about one fifth of a banana, a shot glass of milk, or a teaspoon of light butter. Or you could save it all for a big apple once a week. You could even be a high achiever and skip the elective calories altogether. Either way, you had options.

I left that first meeting delirious with motivation and fast-walked through the mall, past the Ruby Tuesday where I'd shared many a spinach con queso with my camp friends, and past the food court where a classmate and I sometimes people-watched over ice cream or an Arby's sandwich. I didn't know that I'd never eat a normal meal or snack in those spots ever again. I just kept walking, a child with a frantic sudden need to change herself into what people told her to be. A desperate exhilaration rushed through me as I headed straight to the parking lot and dove into the quiet of my car to think about my shopping list. *My beautiful, restricted new diet shopping list.* It was a challenge, almost like a game show where I was the contestant and the game was to fill my cart with the lowest-exchange-value food I could find so I could maximize quantity for the least intake. The winner loses the most weight and ends up the most beautiful.

I had never been more excited to go to a supermarket. I'd never paid attention to a food label in my life, but the old me was gone. This was the new nutrition-savvy me, the one who read the back of the container, who wasn't tempted by the stuff with fillings or fat or taste. I grabbed a cart and slowly rolled through the aisles, loading it with sliced turkey, fat-free cottage cheese, melba toast, Special K, and a box of Sweet'N low. I grabbed cucumbers, lettuce and cabbage, and mustard for taste. These would be my staples for the next few months as my journey into disordered eating began. I knew that day I was starting something life-changing. What I didn't know was that there would never be another day of my life when I wasn't tortured by food.

Adrenaline outweighed the emptiness of starvation those first few weeks. My stomach growled, but I growled back louder. The first week I was on Weight Watchers, I fantasized daily about what my new body would look like. I imagined the stores I'd shop in and how I'd look onstage at my camp color-war show. I'd daydream about dancing in my new body and how people would look at me in disbelief at my transformation. I thought about which plus-size clothes I'd get rid of first, which oversize T-shirts I'd load into bags, and which boys might finally like me.

My second weigh-in couldn't come soon enough. I knew I'd lost weight the first week; I could see it in the way my pants fit, but I didn't want to use my home scale to check. I wanted to experience all the excitement of my achievement in one shot, in front of everyone at the meeting. That day at school I tried to eat and drink as little as possible so I'd see the maximum loss on the Weight Watchers scale.

I got to the meeting early and was second in line for the scale, where everyone waited to be publicly disappointed or applauded. A row of women was forming behind me. Some of them were lifers—women who came to meetings and weigh-ins week after week for the camaraderie of other women who had no luck keeping the weight off. They sat in the meetings, laughing and exchanging low-calorie recipes, hoping to find determination, tired of being overweight but not quite willing to use fat-free dressing on their salad. They came each week hoping this would be the one when they'd be motivated to follow the diet, but if not, there was always next week. I was sad for them, even though they weren't sad. They looked happy and had each other, and they didn't seem to really mind not losing weight.

A woman in a turquoise shirt and capri-length chinos took my recording book and opened to the previous week's weight so she could fill in the line for week two. I couldn't wait for the magical new number. I hated the week-one number and just wanted it gone, in my past. She smiled and told me to climb up. I jammed my heels together to dig off my shoes and inhaled deeply before I stood on the scale.

I was down nine pounds. I was euphoric, but I wanted more. So much more.

The next four months were a blur of food math: exchanging, measuring, obsessively watching everything. I tried to be discreet, counting points and measuring privately so that no one—including my family—would worry. I didn't want anyone to tell me to slow down or throw me off course, not that I would have cared. Weight melted off. I was great at finding options to keep it exciting: exchanging turkey for grilled chicken, exchanging cottage cheese for fat-free ricotta. I swapped cornflakes for bran flakes and dressing for vinegar. I boiled cabbage in water and poured Sweet'N Low on top for dessert. The Weight Watchers guidebook was my bible.

A few weeks after I started my diet, I had a flashback to childhood. I was standing in the middle of JFK airport, about eight or nine years old, with my father's suitcase and carry-on bags emptied all over the airport floor. My father was on Weight Watchers, and as we were checking in for our flight to St. Maarten, he became hysterical about his missing Weight Watchers exchange guide. "I won't fucking know how to exchange anything," I remember him screaming as he maniacally searched through all of his shit that lay scattered on the floor and onlookers stared at the scene. I had never understood why he got so crazy about a book. I'd never understood why someone would need to exchange food. But now I suddenly understood all of it.

My sizes dropped, to 20, then to 18, then to 14, and then to 10. I discovered noncaloric alternatives for regular foods, like zero-calorie condiments that tasted like melted plastic and made me double over in gastrointestinal distress. And butter spray. Lord, how I *loved* low-calorie butter spray. It wasn't really made of butter, it was water and xanthan gum and other flavored chemicals, but I didn't care. It tasted rich and looked like it could have been made of butter, and most importantly, it had hardly any calories, so I didn't use up other exchanges. Sometimes I'd spray it on my finger and lick it off as a snack that I counted toward my elective calories for the week. I left for college nearly fifty pounds lighter than when I'd stood on the doctor's scale four months earlier.

Everyone told me how great I looked.

Everyone was so proud of me.

Just wait, I wanted to tell them. *You ain't seen nothing yet.*

CHAPTER THREE

ALMOST PERFECT

can still smell the stench of the fat-free honey mustard dressing that I kept under my dorm-room bed during freshman year. It didn't smell like honey or mustard—more like a spoiled-mustard-flavored scent—but it didn't taste as gross as some of the other diet dressings I had tried. Plus, I had gotten used to it since I'd started using it as part of my Weight Watchers regimen a few months earlier. So, when I moved to Boston in August 1994, I brought a dozen bottles of the dressing with me and kept them hidden in a box under my bed with all the other diet products that I was scared to live without.

I was sure that none of the other freshmen had brought anything like this to school—it's not exactly comfort food—but I tried not to care. During the first days of college, as I walked through the halls of my freshman housing, meeting my neighbors and scanning the decor of their shared little spaces, the only foods I saw were small bags of candy or chips lying around casually, not hidden away like a dirty secret. *I'm the only one stashing diet mayo under my bed.* In most of the girls' rooms, there was an endless stream of glossy pictures taped to the walls and mirrors, pictures filled with groups of normal-weight teenage girls with their arms around each other, enjoying the types of events that I never went to with my friends— laughing on a beach, wearing sexy matching Halloween costumes, bundled up at a high school football game as they held each other tight. They all had good hair and smiles so big that I could almost feel how great it probably felt to be them, to be pretty and have the life of acceptance that comes with not being fat. I didn't have those kinds of pictures taped to the wall in my room. I didn't have that kind of life in high school.

But no one at my new school would have to know that. When I packed up my mother's car and drove to Boston, I was leaving the old me behind. I couldn't run away from the old me fast enough, with her sloppy body and frumpy clothes, and the way she envied all the prettier girls, wishing she, too, was going to parties and getting attention from boys. I could start over here, where no one knew who I was. In Boston, I could be one of those girls, I told myself, no matter what I had to do to get there. I could be the girl with killer self-control and willpower for days. Whatever had broken me in high school, I could fix it in college. But it would take commitment.

When I arrived in Boston, I was still high off my senior-year slim-down and all the praise from my classmates and camp friends. I certainly wasn't thin, but I wasn't obese anymore, and people in my hometown couldn't help but notice. Everywhere I went, people told me I looked great. "Look at you," said my friends at summer camp. "Way to go," said the trainers at the new gym I joined. But that high, and all the praise, faded fast—in Boston, I was just another chubby freshman. I rushed a sorority, made some great friends, and tried to stop thinking about weight long enough to have some actual fun. And I did have fun, lots of it, but weight dominated my thoughts at all hours of the day and night. All the fun times were tainted with self-doubt, every good time tarnished by the way I hated my body. I compared myself to everyone I saw, other sorority girls, the girls in my classes, the girls in my dorm, the girls at frat parties. I looked at who was thinner, who was fatter, who was having *more* fun because they looked better than I did.

I wanted people to like me, and after four years of feeling like a high school outcast, I wanted people to think that everything about me was normal. I tried to keep my horde of diet products hidden from everyone at school, so they wouldn't think I was weird or obsessed with food, even though I was definitely obsessed with food. The box under my bed held more than bottles of fat-free condiments. It held secrets about who I truly was—a girl infatuated with the idea of being thin, a girl who needed these crappy products stockpiled around her to feel safe eating, a girl incapable of being flexible with her toppings for fear her entire health regimen would fall apart. I didn't want people to think I was that girl, even though I very much was.

I took a small plastic bottle of 20-calorie honey mustard dressing everywhere with me, wrapped in a little plastic bag and hidden in my backpack, and discreetly pulled it out when I went to the dining hall to eat. Then I'd store it in the back of the mini fridge I shared with my roommate, a quiet girl with a fondness for Disney who asked no questions about my diet habits. None of the friends I made freshman year seemed weirded out by the way I ate, either. "Why do you bring dressing with you?" they'd ask matter-of-factly as I poured it over my dining hall salad. "I'm trying to be good," I'd say, "and I'm really into health." That seemed to be enough for them. One time a friend asked to try the dressing before declaring it the worst thing she had ever tasted.

One day some friends from my co-ed dorm came to hang out in my room, among them a jokester named Chris. Chris flung himself on my floor in a fit of laughter over a joke, then peered under my bed. I didn't see him pull the box from underneath, but I felt my heart stop when I turned to catch him riffling through it seconds later. "What the hell is this?" he asked, pulling out one of the bottles as I stood dumbfounded, wholly unprepared to explain what he had discovered. "Just my stuff," I mumbled nervously while he opened a bottle of honey mustard dressing, took a whiff, and then poured the dressing onto my bed. I watched in horror as the light brown contents of half the bottle dripped off my blanket and sheets and onto the floor. "I just wanted to taste it," he said through bellowing laughter while I scrambled to close the bottle and put away the box before anyone could look at what else was inside. My friends called him an asshole, but he didn't care; he clearly thought this was among the funniest things he'd ever done. I tried to clean up the mess, but the smell never came out of my bedding, even after I washed it twice—the sour scent crept into the air around my pillow night after night until I finally asked my mother to ship me a new bed-in-a-bag. The odor was so bad, like if you left a regular dressing in a dirty sneaker until it rotted. It smelled like a toxic diet; it smelled of desperation.

I tried to be "good" in Boston—I tried so hard not to cave in to my hunger—but college threw too many curve balls. I was suddenly out in the world, and there was food everywhere I turned. There were dining halls cluttered with masses of comfort foods, pizza stores and sandwich shops at every turn, ice cream spots and coffee shops and convenience stores littering the streets around campus, and then there was the nightlife. I had never had a nightlife before, and here I was immersed in a world of bars and parties loaded with shitty food and tons of beer and slugs of cheap syrupy liquor and kids chanting for you to take a shot or chug a beer. There were late nights with store runs and drunk kids with newfound freedom, a pocketful of cash, and impaired judgment, stuffing down chips and candy and boxes of cookies as midnight snacks. There were kids taking bong hits everywhere I went, then ordering takeout and eating away their munchies like it was their last meal. My head was spinning with temptation and self-loathing. I counted food exchanges frantically all day, trying to cling to my Weight Watchers routine with bowls full of lettuce in the dining hall. My mind reeled in the food court on central campus as I tried, day after day, to find something diet-approved at the chain eateries that encircled the tables and chairs of hungry students. Sometimes I'd walk from counter to counter, searching for a meal that felt safe enough, until all the time I had left for lunch was gone. I observed what other people ate, who ate more than me or less than me, and I watched enviously as they were able to naturally stop eating midmeal. I wondered how someone could just *leave* over half of a piece of pizza or half a cup of ice cream. *Is that natural? Am I the only one disgusting human who's always compelled to clean her plate?* I tortured myself with guilt and judgment.

Papers listing all of my food exchanges were stuffed into the backs of my notebooks and folders as I tried to hold on to the discipline I'd become so proud of, the discipline I desperately needed to maintain so I could keep running away from the girl I was in high school. But almost every night, I'd fall apart. I would bend to temptation as our nights out grew long, and I'd devour chips and alcohol and snacks and wake up in a fog of self-hatred and regret; then I would try to run five miles in a frantic attempt to make up for my weakness. In the months before college, I had created a contained world for myself, a world centered around Weight Watchers, with no exposure to cravings or interruptions to my schedule, with time to devote to my new, intense exercise regimen, but college was the Wild West. I couldn't figure out how to lose weight there. As hard as I tried, I could only gain it back. Despite all the ways I punished myself, it was coming back.

Within a day of my last freshman final, I went back to New Jersey and back to the Weight Watchers center at the mall by my parents' house. I breathed relief as I walked back in and found myself surrounded by the safety of its pamphlets and charts, its weekly weigh-ins and suggested snacks. "I need to sign up again," I said quietly at the front desk, disgusted with myself and embarrassed that I'd let myself go the way I had. But I was ready to commit once more to the gospel of the Weight Watchers pamphlets. I stepped back on the same scale from a year before, inhaled a deep breath, and took in the number I'd go to war with now. It was lower than high school, but I had still failed, gaining back 20 of the 50 pounds that I'd lost before school. I gave myself no compassion at all, and heard only an inner voice filled with self-loathing: *You fucking pig, all that work for nothing. You just can't deny yourself anything.*

Maybe the worst part was that I hadn't even enjoyed a single bite of anything that made me gain the weight back. I wish I had enjoyed it. I wish I'd gained it all because I'd decided to just let go and have fun in college and not stress about weight, and that I had told myself I'd clean it up over the summer. I wish I'd realized that my new friends loved me, and it had nothing to do with my weight, and they couldn't care less about the size of my pants. But it didn't happen like that at all. Instead, I beat myself up ferociously over every bite I took and then tried to jog it off until my legs felt like they'd break. Food and guilt tasted the same. I lost all 20 pounds that summer and committed to staying the course my sophomore year. *You got this, Jackie,* I told myself as I packed my bags to return to school. *This time you're ready.*

I planned to live in an on-campus suite with five of my closest friends. None of them had issues with weight or food, as far as I knew, and though they'd gladly grab pizza on the way home from a bar, none of them ate with abandon or kept loads of fattening foods in their rooms. My plan was simple: avoid late-night temptation. If I could resist buying food on the way home at night, and go to sleep when we got back to the suite, I could diet successfully. Avoiding temptation was key. But just before school started, one of our intended roommates transferred, and the university assigned a freshman to live in our suite.

Our new roommate, Jessica, quickly became one of my best friends. Jessica was a dancer, with arms and legs of pure muscle, abs lining her flat stomach, and a penchant for late-night food. There were snacks everywhere, there were chips and cookies and pastries, and Jessica would pull them out at night when we'd get back to the suite, and I'd watch her eat as my mind reeled with temptation. I'd sit in the common room, promising myself I wouldn't bend, before stuffing my face with her goodies. Long after Jessica finished taking the few bites she wanted, I was eating the crumbs. I hated myself intensely. All the weight I'd lost from the summer slowly found its way back to my body. It wasn't her fault, of course, but I couldn't handle watching her eat. It made me angry that she could eat all that garbage and stay so lean, and that she knew how to stop after a few bites without tearing through the bottom of the package and shaking the scraps into her mouth. If the average person was a yo-yo dieter, I was a fucking boomerang, flailing out of control between restraint and indulgence, between discipline and mayhem, swinging wildly through 20-pound fluctuations, and sprinting through the streets of Boston to punish myself for my failures.

One morning that fall, I ran through Boston for an hour on an empty stomach, then stripped off my sweat-soaked clothes to weigh myself in my room. I pulled the scale out from under my bed and prayed to the diet gods for a good number. *Please let it be lower than last time, please let it be lower than last time.* I stepped on the scale, opened my clenched eyes, and saw that I had gained another pound. As I stood there in disgust, squeezing the bottom of my stomach and wishing I could cut it off with a knife, Jessica knocked on my door. I threw on a shirt and let her in as she ate from a green box of SnackWell's cookies. As we talked, she stepped casually on the scale that I'd left out by my bed. "I lost a pound," she said with pleasant surprise and the box still in her hands, then continued the conversation like nothing had happened. "Wait, that doesn't make sense," I shouted, in a state of agitation and envy. "How did you lose weight?" Jessica looked at me, confused, probably trying to understand what her weight had to do with mine and why I seemed upset with her. "All I do is exercise and diet, and then YOU lose weight," I cried. Jessica stared at me, speechless, unsure how to respond. "I don't know," she said softly. "I wasn't trying to lose weight. I'm sorry."

Gaining weight didn't keep me from forming manic crushes, as I always had. Dave was a junior in a popular frat. He was tall and funny and cute enough, and after he drunkenly flirted with me on a couch at a party, I was enamored with him. No one had ever really flirted with me, so when it occasionally happened, even when it was just a boy being nicer than usual, I would fall hard. I knew he was too cute for me—frat guys liked slim girls, and I wasn't even close to slim—but everyone I'd ever liked had been too cute for me, including the dozens of crushes I'd had in my fourteen months at college. I asked Dave to go to my sorority formal with me in November 1995, and since a bunch of Dave's frat brothers were going to the formal with my sisters, I figured he'd say yes because of that alone. And I was right.

From the second he said yes, I started sweating over how to look pretty enough not to disappoint him. *Maybe he'll kiss me if I can make myself look pretty enough, if I can find a dress that hides my body. How can I look beautiful for Dave?* I tried everything I could to make myself good enough. I had my makeup done at Lord & Taylor and my hair styled at a chic salon on Newbury Street. I bought a black dress and heels and a new perfume that the saleswoman said her husband found irresistible. *Maybe the perfume will make Dave forget about my weight and make me irresistible,* I thought. But none of it was enough to make him like me, even for one night. I lost track of Dave an hour into the dance, before I found him in the bathroom making out with a freshman. I cried like it was the end of a thirty-year marriage, but I wasn't really crying over Dave. I was crying over me. I couldn't run away from me, no matter how far I ran.

I met Ben a few months later, through one of my sorority sisters who had gone to high school with him. When Ben came to visit her at BU, we locked eyes and connected instantly. We were two chubby Jewish kids looking for love, and we found comfort in each other. I'd never had a boyfriend before, no one who liked me as much as I liked them, and I don't think he'd ever had that, either. Even though we went to different schools, just across the border in different states, Ben was my boyfriend for my junior and senior years. We were in love, I think, but we were lazy, spending weekends bumming around our student apartments, watching movies and eating snacks until we'd leave for a big dinner or to drink our way through the campus bars. I felt no pressure from Ben to lose weight, but I wished I had a boyfriend who would push me to work out with him sometimes, or who wanted to diet with me. It was too easy to be sloths together, and though I finally felt wanted, I also felt disgusting in my skin.

It was on Ben's couch in 1996, watching TV on a lazy afternoon, that I laid eyes on the thinnest woman I think I had ever seen. Fiona Apple was eighteen years old in the video for her song "Criminal," in which she writhes around in various stages of undress as she moves through a dark basement, singing about the sins of infidelity she's committed against the man who loves her. In one poignant scene, Apple sits knee to chest on a kitchen counter, wearing a white satin camisole and shorts with high socks and not a visible ounce of fat on her body. With an agonized look on her exquisite face, she slowly removes her clothes as she stands in the kitchen, running her hands over her tiny abdomen, singing her hit song. Every part of her skeleton, from her prominent hip bones to her bony shoulders and the ribs above her child-size waist, moved dramatically as she stripped down to nothing, the light capturing her sullen blue eyes. She turned away from the cameras, showing off the way her back bones jutted through her skin. *Heaven help me for the way I am / Save me from these evil deeds before I get them done.*

I stared at her on the screen, mesmerized. She was so striking, so desirable, men were throwing themselves at her. She was alluring even when she did nothing but stand in place. She was mysterious in a way I never was. She was dark and enigmatic, the opposite of everything I appeared to be. I wore all my weaknesses on my body. No one had to wonder how I dealt with temptation because my body gave away my whole story: clearly, I dealt with everything by eating. But not this woman. *She's so thin, how does she stay so fucking thin?* I wanted to be mysterious and seductive, tearing the clothes off my skeletal frame because I was so tempting, so consumed with all the love and attention being offered to me, that I couldn't even think about food. I hated how much I wanted to look like her, exactly like Fiona Apple. I had never seen anything more beautiful in my entire life.

Ben accepted my body for what it was, but *I* couldn't accept it for what it was. I had gained back roughly 30 of the 50 pounds I had lost before college, and I was on an endless quest to lose it, but that was impossible while I was with him. I spent my college years continuing my cycle of dieting, hating myself, cursing my thighs and waist, and comparing myself to every girl I saw. In the last few months of college, before I'd graduate and move to New York City to start law school at Fordham, I was determined to lose weight again, and there was only one way I knew how to do that. I needed to find a Weight Watchers.

Downtown Boston felt worlds away from the academic bubble of where I lived near Kenmore Square, with its college bookstores and karaoke bars. But by that point, I would've traveled anywhere for Weight Watchers. I never considered joining a diet program in Boston, for many reasons, but mostly because I was embarrassed. God forbid someone saw me leaving a place known for helping overweight middle-aged housewives trim their gut. I didn't want to be judged or mocked or ostracized the way I had been in New Jersey. I needed to be a different person than I was at home, which meant that some things, like Weight Watchers, couldn't be a part of my life here. Plus, I was so busy at school, between law school applications, sorority obligations, homework, and parties, I didn't have time for weekly weigh-ins and meetings. But I woke up one morning my senior year and realized I'd never lose enough weight to be happy in New York unless I took immediate action. And so here I was.

As foreign as downtown Boston felt, I was grateful to be in an area of the city where I wouldn't run into anyone I knew. I wasn't proud of needing a diet program, which seemingly screamed that I couldn't control myself around food, but I felt I had no choices left. I stepped off the T at Boylston station into a maze of buildings and offices. I walked in circles, searching for the right street to turn down, studying the printed map in my hands, before stopping on the sidewalk of Tremont Street in confusion. I stood still, scanning the windows around me for signage. A uniformed man in his forties stood outside the entrance to a nearby door. "Can I help you find something?" he asked.

I shook my head. "I'm fine," I said, too embarrassed to tell him what I was looking for, until I realized he might be the only one who could help me. "Actually, I'm looking for Weight Watchers," I said matter of factly. *Screw this guy, I'll never see him again.*

"I can direct you there," he said, "but can I talk to you first?" *I don't want to talk to you, I have nothing to say to you,* I thought, but he had military badges on his suit, and I got nervous and didn't say a word. Maybe he sensed my desperation or could see the hopeless look in my eyes as I walked the streets searching for a place to lose weight. I looked at him, and he started to speak. "What if I told you that I could get you into the best shape of your life?"

I stepped inside the glass doors to the military recruitment center and sat in a chair across the desk from the uniformed man as he began to ask me questions about my life. He asked my age, citizenship status, and education level, and I answered everything honestly. I told him I had no criminal background, no history of drug abuse, and aside from my weight, no medical conditions that I knew of. "You seem like a great candidate for service," he said as he pulled out glossy pamphlets and informational packets to share.

I sat nervously in my chair, wondering what the hell I was doing there.

Maybe this is what I need, I thought. *Maybe it's the only thing that can fix me.* I watched his lips move as he preached about the ways that military service would change my life, my confidence, my belief in myself, and the path of my future. I nodded to the rhythm of his words, but none of them actually mattered to me. The only thing I cared about was how military service would change my body. I listened as he talked and talked, and I dreamed about how I might look after basic training, how I'd never worry about temptation again because I'd have discipline coming out of my fucking ears. *Jackie, get the hell out of here NOW, before you do something you can't take back. Get out!*

I took the papers and the pamphlets and thanked him for everything before forcing myself back out onto the city streets. I thought about basic training as I made my way to the Weight Watchers office, shaking at how close I had come to committing my life to the service of my country, all in the name of losing weight. *Why can't I just be a normal person and eat like a normal fucking person? Why does Fiona Apple get to be so goddamn perfect and I have to be like this?*

Weight Watchers didn't feel the same in Boston as it had in New Jersey. There was no excitement this time, only fear that I'd never lose back what I'd gained and annoyance that I had to be at Weight Watchers while my friends were being normal college kids. Although I was relieved to sign up again, filled with renewed hope as I thumbed through the shiny white booklets in the safety of my apartment, that hope wasn't enough to sustain me, and eventually my plans fell apart. It felt like a chore to secretly go all the way downtown and back every week, praying that nobody would find out where I was going. I didn't even tell Ben about joining Weight Watchers, though I'm sure he would've told me I was being silly and that I was beautiful at any size. I was ashamed of how much I hated my body, and I was sad that he loved me so much more than

I loved myself. Everything about sneaking off to a diet program felt shameful, and being on Weight Watchers during college felt like a punishment: I'd have to watch my friends eat and drink freely while I followed a set of rules about exchanges and food values. I lasted only a few weeks before I gave up and never went back. It was too hard to follow a strict diet plan in the face of so much temptation, at a time when I was eating in food courts and cheap restaurants and was expected to drink and party four nights a week. I couldn't control myself the way I needed to in that environment. Sometimes I thought about the military recruitment center, but I never returned there, either.

By the time I arrived in New York a few months later, I was ready to try reinventing myself once again. New York was everything I'd imagined it would be, with beautiful buildings, sexy restaurants, and endless numbers of healthy people jogging through parks and doing yoga in fancy gyms. I vowed to be one of the people who ran through parks. I broke up with Ben as law school was starting, and found another boyfriend for a while, but it did nothing for my self-esteem. I hadn't lost much weight with Weight Watchers senior year, so I was still overweight and obsessed with dieting. I started trying new diets to see what might stick, but nothing ever did. I cycled through the Atkins diet, the South Beach diet, and the Zone diet, among others, but they were all too much work and had too many rules on top of the pressures of law school. I didn't have enough space in my head to manage everything.

Law school was as hard as I'd heard it would be, and like nothing I'd experienced before. Most of my first-year classes at Fordham Law used the Socratic method, in which the professor cold-called on one student and grilled them, sometimes for the entirety of the class session, testing the limits of their preparation as though they were being cross-examined during trial. You had to be prepared; you had to know and understand all the material or risk being embarrassed in front of your peers, admonished by your professor, and appearing subpar in comparison to the very people you'd be competing with for interviews with the country's most prestigious law firms and judges. The competition in law school was fierce, the workload was endless, and the pressure I put on myself was intense. I wanted to make my parents proud—my mother made no secret of how badly she wanted me to be a lawyer—but I also wanted an achievement I could feel proud of, because I was never truly proud of myself. Every sense of accomplishment I'd felt since high school had been shrouded in self-criticism, every momentary success collapsing into sadness over the way I felt about my body. I wished I were one of those people who lost their appetite when they were anxious and felt the weight of the world on their shoulders, but I wasn't. The stress of law school made me want to eat all the time.

I joined a gym near my school and, instead of eating lunch, spent my afternoon break between classes taking giant steps on a staircase machine. On weekends, I ran in a heavy sweatshirt through the streets near my apartment, and I filled my kitchen with diet foods—anything I could eat without gaining weight, even if it made me physically ill, like chips made with Olestra. In 1998, the snack gods blessed consumers with this "miracle" fat substitute that *felt and tasted* like actual oil but with *no fat and no calories*, since its synthetic makeup couldn't be absorbed or digested by the body. And then Frito-Lay went and made my fucking dreams come true by making Olestra Ruffles, Tostitos, and Doritos with half the calories and no fat! I didn't care that every bag had a giant FDA warning about abdominal cramping and loose stools. I didn't mind that the chips sometimes made me so sick to my stomach that I'd race to the bathroom to avoid the "anal leakage" everyone talked about, where giant globs of oil came out of your body and you'd stare into the toilet wondering about what the hell you just ate. Frito-Lay marketed the chips under the brand name WOW!—as in "Wow, these fucking chips make me want to wear Depends" and "Wow, this stuff cannot be good for me." To absolutely no one's surprise, the chips were pretty much gone from shelves within a few years, forcing me to move on to other fake foods to keep from gaining weight. I missed Olestra, and I missed eating chips all day without guilt, but Wow, I didn't miss the side effects.

I tried everything to kill my appetite, like drinking gallons of water and coffee and Diet Coke, but I couldn't resist my hunger. My college friends had moved to the city as well, and when I wasn't studying, I was out constantly at bars and cheap restaurants, the same temptations keeping my weight and self-loathing intact. I watched people wherever I went, looking at their bodies, studying how they ate and what kinds of exercises they did, so I could figure out how they stayed thin.

In department stores, I noticed the way women's clothing fit them, how their shirts tucked into their trousers without bulges or round stomachs pushing their way through. When I went to bars and clubs, I watched twentysomethings with lean frames in slinky clothes fending off advances from men, accepting free drinks, arms above their heads dancing as their shirts rose above their waist to reveal tight stomachs and ribs. I couldn't stop watching people, wishing I looked like them. *I'll figure it out one day, how to look more like them and less like me.*

By 1999, a year after I moved to New York, Tasti D-Lite frozen dessert shops had begun popping up all over the city, and I had officially found my next diet. The brand claimed to make soft-serve ice cream–ish desserts with anywhere from 11 to 17 calories an ounce, depending on the flavor, as opposed to ice cream's typical 60 calories per ounce. Tasti D-Lite's machines pumped air into their soft serve to increase the volume and keep the calories low; the more air they pumped in, the lower the calories in the resulting product.

I decided to go on a Tasti D-Lite diet, and here's how it went: for close to four months, I ate Tasti D-Lite frozen dessert for every meal I possibly could, including breakfast, lunch, dinner, and snacks. I visited as many different shops as I could throughout the city, so I wouldn't have to buy too much from one location at any given time, and I could stock up on enough to fill my freezer with tons and tons of diet soft serve. I didn't care what chemicals were in it, what the flavor was, or how devoid of nutrition it was, I just cared that I could eat "ice cream" all day long and still be on a diet.

I thought if I could spread out my visits to each shop two or three times a week, buying just a few quarts each time, it wouldn't look so suspicious. "Are you having a party?" the guy behind one counter asked me as I took three quarts from the freezer. "Yes," I replied, "I'm having a party. Everyone loves this stuff." He smiled and rang up my order, but the next time I came in, he asked me the same question: "Another party?" I bristled with embarrassment. *Why the hell do you care? Why are you trying to embarrass me?* "Yes, another party," I said with a shy smile. "I love to host parties. Everyone always comes to my place," I babbled. He rang my order and I left, knowing I could never return to that location. *How many parties could I possibly host with buckets of this stuff?*

But as I kept buying quarts of Tasti D-Lite around the city, people in different locations started asking questions, and I'd have to keep answering with excuses. "My whole family loves it," I said sometimes. "My roommates always ask me to get it, since I have the easiest schedule" other times; "I have four roommates and they all love it." In the privacy of my apartment, where I lived alone, I ate from quart containers of Tasti D-Lite, each of which held about 400 calories' worth of creamy fake crap that tasted like heaven compared to the dry-turkey-and-celery-heavy diets I was used to. I reasoned that it wasn't so different from the diets of the eighties, like the cabbage diet or the grapefruit diet, in which you would eat just one food the entire day. So I started every day with coffee and a half quart of Tasti D-Lite, ate a quart for lunch and a quart for dinner, and searched stores for other diet products when I wasn't at home. My stomach pains were sometimes unbearable. I'd be doubled over for hours, with cold, artificially flavored substances rising through my esophagus as my abdomen distended through my pants, sick to my stomach from the nutritionless air I was eating all day and all night so I could look like the type of woman I knew I could be.

But it didn't work. Probably because, as some later testing showed, Tasti D-Lite often had *way* more calories than advertised. If eating tubs of frozen air had made me skinny, then the dreadful cramping and total lack of nutrients would've been worth it to me back then. But I didn't lose any weight at all, so I knew I had to give it up. Plus, the questions from the store clerks were as unbearable as the stomach pains, so I was relieved to be done with that diet. I went back to fad diets and over-the-counter diet pills like Dexatrim, which promised to curb appetite and burn fat, and spending hours at the gym, trying anything and everything to change how I looked. Nothing worked, not even the diet pills, but I wouldn't give up. *I'll figure it out one day,* I kept thinking. *One day something will stick.*

When I thought about my life after law school, I envisioned showing up to my high-powered job in crisp tailored suits, my collars opened just enough for a peek at the sultry lady underneath but closed enough to remind everyone I was a serious woman, a legal superstar in the making. I pictured myself walking the halls of my gigantic law firm, folders in hand, turning heads on my way to a boardroom to do important work. The plan was to immerse myself in so much work that food would be a mere afterthought and, of course, I'd lose weight.

That vision couldn't have been more off. My corporate legal career was comprised of me showing up exhausted to push paper and run highlighter across documents, praying that I didn't get the inevitable four p.m. call from a senior associate telling me I'd have to work late or through the night. I ate whatever crap came across my desk and had dinner in a boardroom three nights a week, ordering from Seamless and reading documents until the sun came up. The gym became a weekend activity, and when I wasn't working late, I was hitting the bars with my college friends, drinking beer and eating nachos at New York institutions like El Rio Grande and Joshua Tree. And those crisp tailored suits? They were more like an array of button-downs and trousers from Banana Republic and Ann Taylor:

cute but not exactly powerhouse fashion statements. Though I immersed myself in work, I certainly didn't lose weight, and I hated my job. After less than a year in the mergers and acquisitions department of a major law firm, I left to do family law at a small but prestigious Park Avenue office.

I thought family law would be a calmer career, one where I could make a difference by helping families make the right decisions for their children, and help people move forward with their lives. I didn't realize I was stepping into the most contentious of worlds—wealthy New Yorkers getting divorced. You've never seen volatile until a rich old millionaire decides to trade in his wife for a younger model. I saw so many devastated women and aggravated men every day that I could barely breathe under the weight of their pain. But the camaraderie of my office was a great distraction. Of the three junior associates, all young women around my age, one of them, Lauren, became a close friend. And of the three partners at the firm, I got close to one, a divorced man in his fifties who was equal parts fun-loving and obnoxious grump. We'll call him Neil.

Neil was the partner I answered to for everything, the one who gave me assignments and checked my work, who would ring my office at nine a.m. from his house in the Hamptons to make sure I was at my desk on time. Neil would get under my skin like no one ever had before, criticizing my work in a way that felt demeaning and nasty, but I also sensed that he wanted to see me succeed. He gave me important assignments and trusted me in court on critical issues. Sometimes we had a nice rapport, talking like peers or having lunch together near the courthouses downtown. Sometimes Neil would massage my shoulders if he came from behind to talk to me, but he never made other advances, so I never said a word. *Besides, why would he want to hit on someone like me, when thin beautiful divorcées walked through the office day in and day out?* A lot of people thought Neil was an asshole, especially other attorneys in New York. His name often made other lawyers crinkle their nose in disgust.

As work wrapped up one evening in early 2003, Lauren and I planned to go out for drinks. I walked into the hallway and stood by her office door, noticing her lean frame and stylish sweater and slacks. "I hate my outfit," I told her, looking down at my heathered beige trousers and striped button-down. My boobs were stretching the material around the buttons of my shirt. "I should go home and change. I can meet you out."

Lauren shook her head as she pulled the rubber band closed on an enormous brown folder and walked out into the hall. "Stop, you don't need to change," she said. "You're perfect."

"Almost perfect," said Neil from his office, about ten feet from where we stood; he was listening to us through his open door. We looked at him, confused, but he looked back only at Lauren.

"Jackie's almost perfect," he said without a trace of a smile on his wrinkled face. "If she lost some weight, she'd be perfect." He looked at me for a split second before looking back down at the papers on his desk, and he didn't say another word.

Lauren and I walked out of the office silently, and once we were safely out of earshot, she touched my arm. "He's an asshole," she said, "don't listen to his shit." My heart dropped through my chest. Lauren looked at my reddening eyes. "I think you're beautiful." But it didn't matter what Lauren thought. I knew what the rest of the world thought of me. *You're a fucking joke with that body of yours. Everyone can control themselves except you.*

It was hard to make eye contact with Neil again after that exchange, and I left the firm to do real estate law a few weeks later, but I took Neil's words with me, as hard as I tried to let them go. In the moments after he said them, as I walked through the office hallway, engulfed by one of the lowest lows I'd ever felt, I realized a sad truth about myself. No matter what I did in life, no matter the schools I got into, the degrees I earned or the tests I aced, the cases I won or the friends I made, I'd never feel like a success until I was thin.

I was almost perfect, just like Neil had said. I could really have it all if I could get my shit together. *Stop being such a fucking slob,* I told myself in the days and weeks after Neil's message lodged itself in my head. *You're a smart girl, Jackie. You can be perfect one day. You can have a perfect life. You just have to figure out how to lose weight.*

CHAPTER FOUR

❧

ANATOMY OF A SPIRAL

SUMMER 2003

I was excited about my new diet. I was going to eliminate one food each week, without adding anything back, until the effects of cutting out enough *bad* foods led to weight loss. To kick it off, I picked dessert. It was easy enough, I just wouldn't eat dessert anymore. There was no thinking involved, no choices to make, and nothing else to do. A few days in, I added fried foods to the cut list, just to speed up any potential weight loss.

For week two, I picked cheese, even though I *loved* cheese. But I was single in New York and dying to lose weight. I was going on lots of Jdates, all the rage for single Jewish women back then, but the guys I met didn't seem that interested in chubby girls. Besides, everywhere I looked, the women in New York were thin. I could sacrifice cheese.

The week after that, I cut out egg yolks, then drinks with any sugar. By the end of week three, I had lost a few pounds. *HALLE-FUCKING-LUJAH!!*

Was it really this basic? I could just cut out little things until I lost all the weight I wanted, and then I could decide what to add back in at whatever pace I needed. I didn't have to follow a diet or weigh in at a center or pay someone to log my shit into their records. No more public weigh-ins or ridiculous meetings. *Fuck off, Weight Watchers!* It was August 2003, I was turning twenty-seven years old, and I was finally figuring it out. Life was good.

And then I decided to cut out fat.

After a few weeks, it dawned on me that fat is probably what makes you fat. (Which is utterly and completely wrong, by the way.) It was simple: *If there's a nonfat version of almost everything, why would you ever eat the one with fat?* I was angry for all the time I had wasted eating fat my whole life. *Why didn't someone tell me this years ago?*

I went back to reading nutrition labels the way I did when I was seventeen, when I studied containers to make sure I was maximizing my Weight Watchers exchanges so I could fit the most food into my day regardless of what it tasted like. It was just math: swap everything with fat for the fat-free version, and you'll naturally be eating way lighter and still having all the foods you want. It was really this fucking uncomplicated all along! *It's all about fat!*

I read the back of containers as if they were suspense novels, enthralled by all the different fat content in everyday foods, captivated by the prospect of removing the high-fat traps from my life, and thrilled when I found a replacement with nary a gram. My goal was to stay under two grams a day, which, it turned out, was pretty easy to do.

I made a simple rule, and I followed it to a tee: everything I ate had to be fat-free. From milk to yogurts to packaged cold cuts and sliced American cheese, everything had been replaced with the fat-free version, and that was all I had to do. Zero-fat SnackWell's replaced cookies, and zero-fat Egg Beaters replaced eggs. I dipped fat-free GG crackers into a tub of fat-free cream cheese and scooped fat-free sour cream with my fat-free cucumbers. Everything I wanted, I could have, as long as it was fat-free. And if I couldn't find a fat-free version of what I wanted, I just didn't want it anymore.

But as I started obsessing over nutrition labels, I was distracted by something even better than fat—something that made fat an afterthought and turned the entire notion of losing weight into one beautiful straightforward mathematical equation in which I wouldn't have to eliminate anything from my diet or deny myself a goddamn thing.

That shiny golden nugget was calories.

Of course, I knew about calories already. Calories were that little number on the back of a package that determined whether I could eat without guilt. They were a measure of how bad I was on any given day and how much I'd hate myself the next morning. I'd tried desperately to keep my daily calories low for years, keeping estimates in my head when I'd devour a box of cookies or a bucket of frozen yogurt. But I'd never thought about the actual science of calories in and calories out. I'd never realized how you could play with calories and how much power that little number had.

I had read somewhere that women needed 1,200 calories a day on average to maintain their body weight, so as long as I ate around 1,000 calories a day, I could keep losing weight no matter what I ate. I could eat anything I wanted as long as the total calories I ingested equaled 1,000. For this to work, I needed to track my intake, the same way I had tracked my exchanges for Weight Watchers. I'd been great at it back then, so I knew it wouldn't be a problem. The only real issue was that I didn't know the calories in foods that didn't come in a package with a nutrition label. So my first stop was Barnes & Noble on the Upper West Side of Manhattan.

I hadn't heard of Corinne T. Netzer before, but she became my guru. Netzer was the goddess of all things calorie-related and an expert on food values, and her precisely detailed books would become the center of my life. Back then there were no iPhones or apps to look up nutritional values with a few clicks. You needed books, and Netzer wrote the best calorie books, the ultimate reference guides for counting anything you might put in your mouth, from brand names at the supermarket to loose nuts floating in a plastic bin to fast food at the mall. Netzer gathered all of it and put it neatly into the 928 pages between the beautiful green soft-covered flaps of my new bible. I bought that, along with her *Encyclopedia of Food Values* and a random pocket guide to calories, so I could have a guide with me at all times. I got myself Post-it notes and a small spiral notebook to keep track of everything. And then I started counting. And tracking. Every day, every food, every calorie. Weight started coming off, and by winter, I was a pro, like a walking calculator with a headful of food values. I could count calories in my sleep. I took Post-it notes and a pen with me no matter where I went.

But I started to hit snags. The more invested I got in being precise, the harder tracking my calories became. If I went out to eat with my friends, I wasn't completely sure what I was eating. How should I count the oil the chef used to cook the food? How should

I count the garnish on my salad? How did I know what an ounce was? Was the dressing light? Was the milk low-fat? I studied a deck of cards so I always knew what three ounces of meat looked like. I used body parts, like my fist size and finger length, to learn how to measure foods like bread and broccoli, so I could calculate their values. I bought myself measuring cups and measuring spoons and food scales so I could be precise at home.

The food guides drove me crazy. If one type of balsamic vinegar had 30 calories per tablespoon and another had 10, how the hell would I know which one was which? One book said salmon had 60 calories an ounce and one book said 50, so which was it? How would I know if my tuna was yellowfin or bluefin? Nothing felt safe unless it came packaged with a nutrition label. Dining out became terrifying, so I'd make any excuse to eat at home. I hated the anxiety that came with all of it. But my God, I loved losing weight. I was about a size 12 when I started eliminating foods earlier that year and a size 10 by the time I started tracking calories in late summer. I was a size 8 when the leaves outside started turning gold and every bite I'd take was weighed first on a kitchen scale, and I was almost a size 6 as I moved the food around on my Thanksgiving plate, eating nothing but dry turkey. I hated needing to control everything so ferociously. But in early December 2003, in the dressing room of Bergdorf Goodman, I buttoned myself into size-4 pants for the first time in my life. *A fucking size 4.* I was still a size 6, but in that glorious moment, I was a 4. I was becoming one of those women I never thought I could be. I was becoming skinny.

It's hard to tell someone that you think they have a problem, especially when you're not sure exactly what their problem is, or if there's even a problem to begin with. In a world that values thin bodies and where willpower is a superpower, losing weight is rarely seen as a problem. In a city like New York, where people believe you can never be too rich or too thin, there was nothing visibly wrong with anything I was doing. In fact, the positive reinforcement was almost overwhelming. Clearly, nobody thought I had any kind of issue. And if they did, they never said a word about it to me.

"You look amazing," people would tell me everywhere I went, from work to the gym to the halls of my apartment building. My coworkers marveled at my new physique, and my friends joked that I was wasting away. Men at bars bought me drinks, and at the gym, where I'd started running six miles a day, people envied my determination. "How the hell do you stay on the treadmill that long?" one woman asked me, then joked, "That's why you're thin and I'm not." She kept talking, but all I heard was "thin." I thought, *She called me thin. I can't believe someone called me thin.* The word hung in the air before pouring through my head and into my veins. I stood up straight and wiped the sweat from my lip. I wanted to never not be thin ever again. I wanted even more people to call me thin.

I didn't want to do the calorie counting much longer, but I didn't know how to *not* do it and stay almost thin. If I stopped counting calories, I'd gain it all back; I was certain of it. I resolved to follow my diet until I reached a size 2 and then slowly hit the brakes.

And then I met Evan.

We were at a crowded bar on New York's Upper East Side, the kind of watering hole that was littered with cute twentysomethings in expensive jeans dancing to songs like "Sweet Home Alabama." This particular spot, Brother Jimmy's, was known for its massive fishbowls full of mystery alcohol that came with a bunch of straws so you could share your germs with people you wanted to hook up with. But every Thursday, when I'd go to Brother Jimmy's with my best friend, Hannah, I drank only light beer because I knew the calories in light beer. On December 18, 2003, we sat at the bar while Hannah scanned the menu for food. I saw Evan when I sat down, but he wasn't the type of guy who'd like me. He was too handsome, and with his backward cap, he had that frat-guy look. I was never cute enough for frat guys. "Would you eat frickles?" Hannah asked me, referring to the fried pickles, which were possibly the grossest thing on the menu. "Absolutely not," I said with a laugh. "I'm actually not hungry at all," I lied, "so just order whatever you want." She continued searching the menu as I mentally calculated how much beer I could drink that night, when a voice came over my shoulder. "I hear the filet mignon is excellent." I turned around, and it was him. He was talking to me.

Evan was the most beautiful man who had ever looked at me in *that way*. Evan was tall and lean, with muscular arms, piercing green eyes, and a pack of good-looking friends who would've looked right past me in high school. He was the kind of guy who, by the looks of him, probably would have dated Stef, the most perfect girl in my high school, the one you could pick up with your pinkie. But now he wanted me.

Evan never said a word about my body or my weight when we first dated; he only swept his hands over my size-6 curves and told me I was beautiful. He never talked about wanting a thin woman or what his ex's bodies looked like. But I was terrified that gaining weight at the start of our relationship would scare him away, so giving up my diet wasn't an option yet.

By January, just a month into dating, Evan could tell that something was off with the way I behaved around food.

Sometimes, on cold January nights, I'd go to his apartment to watch a movie on his couch. I was falling in love, blissfully happy, but terrified of losing him. If dropping weight meant finding love like this, I would do anything to keep it going. On those cold winter nights, the only thing I would ever eat were the jelly beans that I brought with me, counted out in a Ziploc bag or a small package. They had to be Jelly Belly, because they were 4 calories a bean, not like the jumbo jelly beans sold in loose bins around the city. As we'd watch a movie, I'd put each one in my mouth, one at a time, and use my teeth to peel the hard layer of sugar off the outside of the bean, leaving just the soft inside part, which I'd roll against the roof of my mouth until I couldn't resist chewing it. A small bag of Jelly Bellys could last an entire movie. I never touched anything else Evan offered, I always came after dinner, and I never wanted to order in. "I'm good, babe. I'm just in the mood for jelly beans," I'd tell him. At first he probably thought I just really liked candy, but it didn't take long for him to see that something wasn't right. "Are you sure?" he started to ask when I turned down food. "Are you sure you can't have a few bites? We can share," he'd say gently. "You can have some, it won't do anything." But I never let him push for too long, and my willpower never wavered. I just repeated "I'm good" over and over until the food disappeared. By February, we were in love, and I was starving.

My memories of dating Evan all bring me back to hiding. Hiding my behavior around food, hiding the counting, hiding my hunger. I was obsessively tracking calories, eating fake packaged diet foods, and measuring things on kitchen scales. I called myself a "health nut" to explain it away. I'd leave in the middle of meals to hide in a bathroom stall and write everything down that I ate. Gaining weight meant going back to who I used to be, and I couldn't let that happen, not yet. I couldn't risk losing Evan.

In March 2004, Evan took me for a movie and dinner. We'd been to the movies once or twice before, so he knew my routine of bringing my own snacks along. I was scared of being hungry and having nothing I could eat, so I always packed tiny portions of snack foods in the smallest Ziploc bags to take with me wherever I went, so I didn't have to buy anything when I was out of my apartment. Movies were hard because everyone was eating around me and it smelled like food, and all the offerings at the concession stand were death traps for a dieter. I was afraid I might break, that I'd get so hungry I'd have to choose between passing out and buying popcorn. By that point, I'd have taken an emergency room over popcorn. The fear of gaining weight and going back to the old me—when I was finally starting to look like the person I'd always wanted to be, when I had finally found the love of my life—was overwhelming. It buried my hunger under layers of panic.

During the movie, I picked through my two little snack bags, one containing tiny cut-up pieces of dried fruit, and the other containing twenty-five jelly beans sliced in half, trying to space out my bites so they'd last the entirety of the movie. As long as I felt like I was eating *something*, no matter what it was, I didn't feel the starvation. After the movie, we headed to dinner.

Dining out started giving me debilitating anxiety. Something I once loved had become completely unenjoyable, and reading menus felt like navigating land mines. I became that person who substituted everything in the meal, because it was all I could do to protect my body. I had developed a system for restaurants that was easy and safe. Plain salad to start, dressing on the side that went untouched, steamed fish with no oil, and steamed vegetables on the side. It was the only meal I could eat out. After dinner, I'd consult my guidebooks for the calories in the fish and write everything down in my spiral tracker. Having systems was the only way to keep all the numbers organized, and every day there were more numbers to keep track of. I had to track the minutes of my cardio workouts also, and of course, I had to precisely track my weight.

Evan's favorite meal was sushi, which was my favorite meal, too, but not because I liked sushi. I didn't care for sushi at all, but sashimi is completely uncooked, which took away any possibility of added fats; edamame is steamed; and oshitashi, a Japanese spinach dish, is steamed, so I never had to worry about oil. By March, the way I ate had nothing to do with hunger or cravings anymore. I didn't eat when my stomach growled with emptiness or have chips when I craved something crunchy. I ate because the clock said I could eat, and I ingested what my ration allowed me to ingest. I told myself it wouldn't go on forever. Once I lost all the weight I needed to lose, once I was sure that Evan loved me enough not to leave if I got fat, I'd work on getting back to normal.

During dinner, Evan asked if I wanted to share a sushi roll with him. "I'm not that hungry," I lied, "this is all I want." In the past few months, he had asked me many times to share food with him, and almost every time, I'd said no. I hated when he asked to share food, because I didn't want to have to say no. I didn't want to draw more attention to the way I ate, I just wanted to get through the meal.

Evan had gotten so used to me saying no to sharing that he didn't even react. He ordered the roll anyway and just ate it all on his own. "You can have some if you want it," he reminded me, pointing to the sushi with his chopstick, knowing that I wouldn't be having any. I just smiled and said thank you and went back to my steamed or raw food.

Evan had spent months watching me graze on food all day, not knowing I was eating nothing of substance. He had no idea what was in those little Ziplocs I'd eaten my way through at the movie, just before we got to the Japanese restaurant. As he ate his sushi, we started talking about sports and the best way to keep your body fueled when you're athletic. Evan had always been an athlete, and though he never dieted or obsessed over nutrition, he tried to make healthy food choices and ate multiple protein bars a day. He told me that it was actually better to have small meals all day instead of three big meals.

"You're doing it right," he said, referencing the two bags of snacks I'd had at the movie, clearly ignorant about the tiny portions they contained. Maybe he was trying to put a positive spin on my diet so it wouldn't seem as strange. Maybe he didn't want me to feel bad about always saying no to food by helping me believe that what I was really doing was fueling my body all day long. "You eat constantly, that's good."

What came next was *not* good. Hearing him tell me that I ate constantly triggered something inside me, as though he had called me fat, as though he could see the overweight person waiting to break out once I stopped starving myself. Suddenly, I was back in high school, obese and unwanted, watching a boy I loved tell me that all I did was eat. I knew I had lost a lot of weight, that I was already thinner than when I'd met him in December, but I was so scared of being seen as the old me that I snapped. I fought back so defensively that he thought we were breaking up.

"How dare you fucking say that to me. How horribly insulting. Who the hell are you to call me fat?"

He apologized several times, but I didn't speak to him again that night. When we spoke the next day, he apologized again for talking about the way I ate, and he didn't dare open his mouth to me about the way I did or didn't eat ever again. We went on like this for a while, my strange eating habits playing out, Evan staying quiet about all of it, and my weight continuing to drop. By the time we had that conversation, the size-4 pants I was wearing were becoming so loose that I'd soon fold them away in the back of my closet, together with all the rest of my clothes that no longer fit.

In May 2004, Evan took me out to see an old friend of his. With every day that passed, Evan and I grew closer, and by late spring, he wanted me to meet everyone in his life. We met Mike at a fun Upper West Side bar for a few drinks. I was getting used to all the counting, and I'd settled into a routine of how to eat, how to count, how to track, how to exercise, so that we could go out all the time and I wouldn't gain weight. Evan and I ran around New York City, young and in love, having the time of our lives, but I lived in a constant state of fear about getting fat. Everything I did, and everywhere I went, my first priority was staying thin. I knew the calories in all the light beers a bar might stock, so I never had to worry about drinking when we went out. I had also designed a system for saving calories, so I could eat at a deficit during the week to save a few hundred calories for the weekends or nights out. *So many different systems.* This particular day, I had saved calories from my daytime meals so I could drink a little more at night and seem normal for his friend.

We stood at the bar talking about everything—Mike's girlfriend, our vacation, his plans, our jobs—and then it all went black. I woke up on the floor, staring up at Evan, in a dizzying mix of embarrassment and confusion. Four people took me by the arms and helped me stand up as everyone in the room watched me. I apologized to Mike, saying I had no idea what happened and blaming it on low blood sugar. "You should probably get home," Mike said, and we left. Evan and I both knew why I had fainted, but neither of us said another word about it.

Despite the weird eating habits and food scales and obsessive exercise, Evan loved me. It was unconditional love, the kind of love that made me believe in soulmates and higher powers. It was the kind of love I'd always wanted and always thought would make me feel worthy after all. Instead, it made me behave worse. The world became black and white, and there were only two options. In one world I was thin, triumphant, and worthy of the love of a beautiful and successful man, and in the other I was heavy and forgettable, wearing dumpy clothes and chasing boys who wouldn't give me a second glance. I was desperate to stay in this world, no matter the price. By the time Evan asked me to marry him, after nearly two years of dating, I was skeletal. I knew I had a serious problem, but I had no idea how to fix it.

My engagement day will always be one of my favorite days, but like every happy day I've had since 2003, it's one that is stained by anorexia. My eating disorder was relentless, and it gave me no days off, not even special occasions. Looking back on happy times is like watching them unfold through a dirty window, where I can see all the good stuff, but I also see the layer of grime on top.

In September 2005, Evan had gone to Germany on a business trip, so my closest girlfriend asked me to join her for the evening. She worked in admissions at a major university and was hosting an event for the business students at the Mandarin Oriental Hotel on New York's Columbus Circle. The Mandarin was a special place for me. Evan and I had gone there for a drink on our third date, a pivotal night when we felt ourselves falling in love. I said yes to my friend but warned her that I'd be coming after dinner and wouldn't be eating. She didn't care about that, probably because she was so used to hearing it from me.

A few blocks down from the hotel was a "health food" store that stocked every diet food you could imagine. Every chip or bar or candy made with strange unnatural sweeteners and weirdo crap, that clocked in at half the calories of the regular stuff, you could find it there.

I decided to make a pit stop at the store before meeting my friend. When I got there, I went straight to one of the products I loved—an incredibly low-calorie black-and-white cookie. I'd already had two of them that day, but this one could be my dinner. I had a tendency to become obsessed with a single diet product that felt safe, like the low-calorie cookie, and I'd eat it as my only snack or meal replacement until I discovered something even lower-calorie and weirder. The cookie was loaded with synthetic shit, but it was kind of decent-tasting, all things considered. I used to eat it slowly, savoring the fake icing and picking apart tiny morsels of the soft cake bottom.

That day in the health food store, there was something unusual about the cookie. Even though the cookie looked the same as usual, I noticed the package looked different, and when I picked it up, I saw that the nutrition label had changed. The sticker on the back used to say 100 calories per cookie, and now it said 100 calories per serving and 2.5 servings per package. The same exact cookie, with the same ingredients, in the same size, was now 250 calories. *It must have been 250 calories all along. Holy shit holy shit holy shit.* Numbers started ripping through my head as I thought about all the damage I had done to my body with these fucking cookies. How do I compensate for this? What do I do what do I do? I thought about the extra 300 calories I had unknowingly had that day and the countless extra calories I must have had that week. The only thing I could do was skip the event and go to the gym instead. I called my friend to tell her I wasn't coming, but she was adamant that I come. "You're not skipping this. I need you there. I'll explain why later, but please don't leave me alone." I didn't understand why she'd need me at her work event, but she was my best friend, and I hated to disappoint her. I would just double my run every day for a few days until I burned off all the extras. I did math in my head the entirety of my ten-minute walk to the hotel, calculating how much running I'd need to do to burn off the extra calories. I was disgusted with myself, but I was also sad. I really loved that cookie. It was the only cookie I could eat.

I met my friend in the lobby of the hotel, and she handed me a card inside an envelope. "That's your invite," she said. "Open it before we get upstairs." My head was still spinning, my mind still doing math. "Why do I need it if I'm with you?" I asked as we got in the elevator. "Just open it," she said as we climbed to the thirty-fifth floor. I ripped the envelope and took out the card, a blank white notecard that said, "I think we've waited long enough." When the elevator doors opened, Evan was on his knee with a ring in his hand.

After the yes and the kisses and tears, the hotel staff set us up in a romantic corner of the bar, the same bar where we'd had our third date, next to windows overlooking the Manhattan night, with champagne awaiting us in tall crystal glasses. I studied my glass. It was taller than normal. I studied it more. *Is it wider, too?* I wrapped my hand around it to see if my fingers met in the same spot they did on my glasses at home. It was the type of glass that easily held 10 ounces instead of 7. I jotted "champ 250" on a Post-it note, put it in my bag, and turned back to my future husband.

As we talked excitedly about our plans, my head kept flashing to those cookies. I took the knife from the small table where the staff had placed a beautiful display of chocolate-covered strawberries. One by one, I carved the chocolate off the fruit, leaving a broken pile of brown shells on the plate, wiped the berries with the napkin from my drink, and ate my dinner of plain fruit. I wondered if the ring would still fit tomorrow, when the cookies started to take effect. I couldn't stop worrying about those cookies.

I had told myself that getting engaged would be a sign that it was time to stop starving myself, but even knowing that Evan wanted to spend his life with me wasn't enough. I couldn't wrap my head around gaining weight. *No one gets fatter before their wedding, that's backward,* I thought. *I'll stop after the wedding, so I can enjoy the honeymoon.*

My mother and I shopped for my wedding dress at one of those upscale Manhattan bridal boutiques that you see in movies. Sitting on a blue velvet chair, she watched as I tried on dresses and twirled in the dressing room mirror, admiring the tall, lean woman staring back at me: a woman who had gone through a long and grueling ugly-duckling phase to emerge a beautiful, successful attorney, preparing to marry the man of her dreams. I knew my mother was proud of me and that she adored Evan. Her eyes welled as she watched me. Her tears were sweet, but I told her not to be sappy. "I'm not crying tears of joy," she said. "I'm scared of how thin you are." She had mentioned her concerns occasionally during the past year, gently telling me not to lose any more weight, carefully saying I was getting too skinny, but this was the first time I'd seen fear in her eyes. It was the first time I'd sensed sadness in her voice as she stared at my bones. On the one hand, it broke my heart to know I was hurting my mother. But on the other hand, it was a stark validation that my diet was still working. I was still losing weight, and that was what mattered. It didn't matter what anyone thought, not even the people I loved, I just needed to stay the course. I looked at myself one last time and took off my dress, quickly grabbing my shirt to hide my concave stomach from my mother.

No one—except my parents—had said anything to me about my weight, but I could tell that it made people nervous. If I ran into someone I hadn't seen in a while, they would pause and stare, unsure of how to react, before saying hello—but no one asked if I was okay or if I wanted to talk. People stopped complimenting me on my body, only mentioning how tiny I'd gotten, but no one asked if I needed help. My dad would say I was getting too thin, which was telling considering his thoughts on weight loss as the most elusive prize and ultimate victory for someone who was once fat. Weight loss, to my father, was proof of willpower and determination, and I'd never once heard him say anyone had lost too much weight. But even he wouldn't press me on the topic, which was a relief. Once in a while, my mother would tell me my arms looked like I'd just come out of a concentration camp. But horribly, the sicker I got, the more it helped to hear that my efforts were paying off. *If you're gonna starve, you might as well look emaciated.* I took her worries as a compliment.

A few weeks before our wedding, Evan and I were sitting on the couch in our apartment when my head started to hurt. Within minutes, I was on the floor with a headache so severe I couldn't see. As I held my head in my hands and my brain pulsed wildly through my scalp, Evan rushed me to the emergency room, from which I was transferred to the Manhattan Eye, Ear & Throat Hospital. I had struggled with sinus issues for years, long before my anorexia started and unrelated to it, as far as I knew, so it was no surprise that the headache had been caused by a massive infection running through my sinuses and inflaming half of my face.

"You have chronic sinusitis. We need to do surgery to clean out your sinuses so it doesn't get worse or happen again," said my doctor, explaining how she'd go in through my nose to drain the congestion and fix whatever was causing the infection. "You'll be in bandages and bruised for a little while," she explained. I could handle that, but I suddenly panicked. *What about exercise? I have to run.* "You'll need to take at least a week off of exercise after surgery," she said, noting that running could cause the incisions to tear from exertion, generating swelling, bleeding, and other trauma, and risking reinfection. "You'll be bandaged, and you'll need to heal." I begged her to wait to do the surgery until after the wedding, which was a few weeks away. "I don't want to be bruised," I told her. But mostly, I couldn't take a week off from the gym. Not now, not with so much planning and anxiety. I couldn't even handle thinking about it. If I had a few more weeks, I could figure out how to do it, but I wasn't ready, and I wouldn't let her talk me into it. She put me on the strongest antibiotics, which alleviated the infection enough to control my headaches, buying me a little more time, and I scheduled the surgery for two days after our honeymoon.

I gave myself permission to spiral before the wedding by promising myself I'd find some kind of help right after. If I could think about food and calories, I didn't have to think about the fights I was having with my parents over every aspect of the wedding or the general stress of planning. So I cut small pieces off of whatever I was eating and threw the pieces away. I added time to the treadmill when I wasn't too exhausted to keep running, and if I found myself relaxing, I got on the floor and did sit-ups. With colored pencils and ruler-straight lines, I made charts to track all the deficits I was building in. When all the planning and fighting made me feel agitated, I found serenity in the control I had over my body, what I put in it and what I took away from it. When I lay in bed in the morning, if I could feel my hand rise a steep, smooth slope from my hollow stomach to the top of my hip bone, I felt safe. *I'll get better after the wedding, I can't do this much longer.*

But the wedding came and went, and I kept going like I did before. Evan gathered restaurant recommendations for Capri, where we spent the first week of our honeymoon. I could tell that he wanted me to ease up on my diet, even for a few days, so he did whatever he could to nudge me into eating. He wasn't trained on how to handle this, on what to do when someone is wasting away in front of your very eyes, on what to say when your new wife is killing herself in front of you but the mere mention of any concern starts a firestorm of reactions. He didn't know when to stop trusting my assurances that everything was fine, that I felt great, that I wasn't hungry. He didn't know how to do any of it, so he just acted like everything was okay, and he prayed that somehow everything would be okay.

Before we left, Evan talked about the pasta they made in Italy, how it would taste different than the pasta at home, how much fresher the ingredients were and how pure the olive oil was. The conversations made me angry and paranoid. *Is this his way of telling me I have to try their olive oil? Is he going to push me to taste the olive oil? I don't want the fucking olive oil, why is he doing this?* I rehearsed conversations in my head so I'd have responses ready for why I couldn't try it or didn't want it or wasn't hungry. I'd stand idly in the shower, running scenarios through my head as water poured over my bones, anxiously anticipating what might happen in Italy. *Why the hell should I feel bad about what I'm putting into my body and the fact that I'm not sharing with him? I'll still be there at the table, I'll sip wine and have a salad, what business is it of his or of anyone's what I put in my mouth?* It made me tense to imagine being challenged when, in reality, no one was challenging me—especially Evan. He

was terrified of my possible reaction, and I'm sure he felt that starting a war was not the best way to kick off our marriage.

Our first night in Italy, we decided to walk the streets and get food
from little Italian grocery stores to eat on our balcony with a bottle of
wine. It could've been really romantic and beautiful, in theory. Back
at the hotel, together on our balcony, I took a round, individual-sized
piece of pizza on a plate, removed the cheese and the sauce, tore the
bread apart with my hands so it looked like I might've eaten some,
and using a fork, I slowly ate just the sauce, picking up bits of tomato
between the silver prongs and sliding them into my mouth as I sipped
from a glass of wine. *You don't need to consume heavy crap,* I told myself of the Italian foods laid out before me. *Being thin means having
self-control.* If Evan was upset that I didn't share the meal with him,
he didn't say a word. It was the best I could do, and maybe he knew
that. Before bed, I checked the calories in tomato sauce using the
nine-hundred-page Corinne Netzer book I'd packed, and logged the
meal of a half cup of tomato sauce into my records. The next ten days
were different sad versions of the same. Different beautiful restaurants, stunning views, and lots of undressed salads as my husband ate
alone. One night we ate at a restaurant famous for its pasta; at Evan's
request, I took one bite out of a bowl of spaghetti so I could give him
hope and I could pretend to be normal. I'm not sure I even tasted it.
I should have savored the pasta, noticed the texture on my tongue,
felt real food moving through my body, but I only thought about the
potential effects of my moment of weakness. *I'll count it as 50 calories.
What a waste of 50 calories.* The waiter took our picture as the bowl
of pasta sat in front of me. Smiling for the camera, I thought I could
show it to people, and maybe they'd think that was what I ate. That

I eat pasta and I'm just naturally thin. *I'll get better when we decide to have a baby. I have time.*

woke up early to run on my treadmill the morning of my surgery, despite having fasted for the anesthesia, because I knew I wouldn't be able to exercise for a week after that. That afternoon, I woke up from the procedure with my swollen face wrapped in bandages and was sent home with instructions for wound care over the next several days, including the warning not to exercise or blow my nose for at least the next week.

The next morning, I got out of bed bruised and congested, my face covered in gauze and tape and my head in a slight fog. I put on workout clothes, waited for Evan to leave for the gym, and walked over to my treadmill. I stood there silently. *I'm not supposed to do this. What if I do this and my incisions open?* I climbed on the treadmill. *Don't do this.* As I started to run, the sweat loosened my bandages, and my nose leaked. The throbbing intensified, and I couldn't tell if it was sweat or mucus or blood that was running down my chin. By the time Evan came back, I had retaped my face, changed my clothes, and lay back down in a fog of pain and relief.

From there, my secrets only got worse and my behaviors more dangerous. My body was in starvation mode, holding on to anything I ate in order to keep me alive, and as my metabolism slowed, weight became harder to lose and harder to keep off. Calories were all I thought about—I had to find more ways to cut them from my diet or to burn them off.

I started freezing all my food so it would take longer to eat. Yogurt,

Staten Island kid, circa 1983.

Celebrating my eighth birthday at the Staten Island Mall with Eric,
October 1984.

Shoved a butterfly clip in my hair for my fourth grade picture. P.S. 36, Staten Island, 1985.

Always playing outside, sometimes with an open fly. Staten Island, New York, 1986.

At my childhood home, ready to play ball. Staten Island, New York, 1988.

Eighth grade picture, I.S. 34., Staten Island, New York, 1989.

No neighbors in sight. On the deck of my new home in New Jersey, November 1990.

My Sweet Sixteen. October 1992.

Junior prom. May 1993.

Senior prom night. May 1994.

Senior yearbook photo. 1994.

Peace out! High School Graduation.
June 1994.

The date who snuck away. Boston,
Massachusetts, November 1995.

Spring break
in Puerto Rico.
March 1997.

Spring break in Miami.
March 1998.

With my boyfriend Ben.
Summer 1998.

Fordham Law School
Graduation. Lincoln Center,
May 2001.

As a young lawyer at
a Park Avenue law
firm. New York City,
February 2003.

Skin and bones at my
wedding shower. New York
City, June 2005.

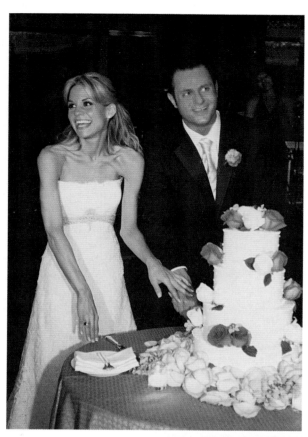

About to cut my wedding cake. Mandarin Oriental, New York City, August 26, 2006.

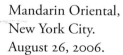

Mandarin Oriental, New York City. August 26, 2006.

Mexico. February 2007.

The pasta picture. Capri, Italy, September 2006.

Starving at the Dead Sea. 2007.

The night before my fortieth birthday. October 1, 2016.

Family vacation to the Dominican Republic. December 2017.

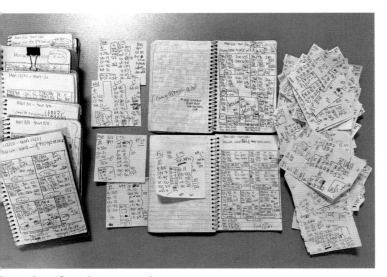

Decades of tracking my calories.

Red Dress Awards with Margaret Josephs. New York City, February 2019.

Backstage at the *The Rea Housewives of New Jersey* reunion. New York City January 2020.

Ready to film an all cast event. New Jersey, March 2019.

Filming with Melissa Gorga at the start of my fourth season. Edgewater, New Jersey, June 2021.

Mother's Day. Piermont, New York, May 2022.

Sailing in Long Island, New York. May 2022.

Long Island, New York. May 2022.

East Brunswick, New Jersey.
August 2022.

Ready for football! MetLife Stadium,
East Rutherford, New Jersey,
September 2022.

Celebrating my forty-sixth birthday. Edgewater, New Jersey,
October 2, 2022.

Date night. New York, New York, December 2022.

Santa Monica Pier, California. December 2022.

Spring break in Miami Beach, Florida. April 2023.

apples, raisins… Nothing was unfreezable, so I froze all of it. Then I could suck and scrape instead of eating and chewing, and I could make a 50-calorie meal last twenty minutes. As an engagement gift, we got a caviar set with a tiny fancy spoon in a tiny fancy bowl. I started using the tiny spoon for meals. I bought mini crab forks with only two prongs to eat my salads with. Anything that could make food last longer, I sought it out. Eventually, I bought sipper straws—the tiny straws that people used to stir coffee—flattened them out with my teeth, and used the three-millimeter edge to eat oatmeal. One plain packet of oatmeal mixed with two cups of water and three packets of Sweet'N Low took me a half hour to eat on the flattened edge of a sipper straw. *When will this end? Please, God, I need this to end.*

How do you tell when you've reached rock bottom if every day is worse than the one before? How can the next day be any worse when every bite today feels like you're throwing your life away? Sometimes I'd wonder what was worse: feeling like a nobody when I was fat or the dizzying crushes of hunger I endured day and night to stay thin. *They're both an emptiness,* I told myself, *but the hunger is just physical, while the worthlessness permeated everything.* In my heart, I prayed for this hell to be over, but in my head, the end of starvation meant going back to the way I was before, living in a body I hated, feeling repulsive to the world, and always wishing I could be somebody else. *I can fight the hunger, but I could never bear the worthlessness. I can keep going.*

I n 2007: "Let's go to Mexico," Evan said at the start of the year. We were newlyweds, crazy in love and eager to leave the cold of New York City. The cold had become unbearable, penetrating my skin and cutting through the layers of blood and minuscule flesh that covered my bones, chilling my insides. I quivered uncontrollably in anything below 50 degrees. My lips would turn blue, like those of a little girl leaving a pool, and my fingers would go numb. The sides of my face and back now had a slightly noticeable layer of blond hair called lanugo, a soft feathery hair that covers newborn babies and malnourished adults to insulate their bodies and keep them warm. When I got cold, those fine blond hairs would stand on end. "Yes, let's go away," I replied.

I wanted Evan to be happy, and I wanted to say yes to every adventure, but traveling was torture. Leaving home for more than a night meant eating every meal out, for any number of days, and there was so much planning, so many numbers, and so much hunger. I spent the next week obsessing over how and what to eat, and made a plan to cover my meals and exercise. I always made a plan.

As I always did before I dined out, I called the hotel to make sure the restaurants would accommodate my extensive dietary requests, but I was told that at an all-inclusive resort, the restaurants wouldn't change the style of cooking. That meant they wouldn't steam anything for me, and unless I figured this out, I couldn't eat anything at all.

I'd never gone on a vacation like that before, where the food was already paid for and you couldn't make changes. Usually, if I had to go to a restaurant—a painful experience to begin with—I changed everything when I ordered my food. No oil touched my fish, no marinade touched my sides, and no sauce touched my plate. I couldn't do any of that here—that control was taken away from me—and it was gut-wrenching. But Evan wanted to go to Mexico, and I so badly wanted to try to be normal on vacation. I wanted to be normal for him because he deserved a normal wife.

"Do you care if I just get two appetizers?" I asked Evan as we opened the menu during our first dinner of the trip. I wore a long green dress with palm prints and a black wool sweater, despite the tropical weather. "Get whatever you want," he said with a gentle smile. I didn't expect him to fight me. Ever since I had bitten his head off at the sushi place years before, Evan tried not to comment on what I ate or how I ate. I ordered two appetizer salads with dressing on the side. The waiter didn't understand my order or why I didn't want any actual food, but I didn't give a shit.

We held hands and talked as the waiter brought our first course, and instantly, my mind flipped. Evan's voice became background noise as I counted how much lettuce and shredded carrot was on my plate and how much crouton dust was touching my tomatoes. I removed the almonds and the orange slices and the precariously placed container of dressing, and searched the salad for any traces of oil. I reached for the thin stack of Post-its in my bag with my running tally of calorie counts for the day, added the calories in the salad, resumed eye contact with my husband, and continued the conversation. I repeated the whole routine when they brought the second salad. As we talked about plans for future trips, I thought about what I could eat for breakfast. "Can you order me tea for dessert?" I asked before excusing myself to use the bathroom.

I walked into the restroom, shut the door on the farthest stall, and quietly closed the cover of the toilet. I placed toilet paper over my lap, pulled a white plastic spoon from my purse, and quickly opened the first of two small cans of premixed 70-calorie StarKist tuna salad I had brought for dinner. I stared at the palm leaves on my dress as I shoveled the tuna into my mouth, letting the food fall deep into my empty stomach, and I felt the hunger start to lift. I tried not to think about anything, letting my mind go blank so I wouldn't cry, so Evan wouldn't suspect anything. If he smelled the tuna or saw running makeup under my eyes, he might try to save me. I wasn't ready for him to save me.

Day after day and night after night, I tried not to cry as I hid in a stall and ate tuna in the different bathrooms of our hotel. I had brought thirty-six cans of premixed tuna salad, packed neatly underneath my clothing in my suitcase and covered in tissue paper, for my four-night trip to Mexico. My plan was simple: tuna for breakfast, and again for lunch, and again for dinner. At some points, I felt like a cat, eating dry meat from a can, which was almost funny in the face of how *not* funny it all was.

Is this rock bottom? And if so, how long can I stay here? Because I don't think I'll ever know how to leave.

I call that trip my lowest point, not because anything changed after that but because when I got home and stood on my scale, I realized for the very first time that I was actually on the way to killing myself. I stared at the number on the scale, well over 100 pounds thinner than I'd been in high school, and I suddenly understood what I was doing to myself. I also understood that I couldn't stop myself. If someone started to tell me I was too thin, I cut the conversation off before it could even start, because I felt incapable of finding my way back. I wasn't sure I wanted to find my way back because of the life that might be waiting for me when I got there. I was on a dead-end road, and I didn't know what to do.

I'm going to die. Please somebody make it stop.

CHAPTER FIVE

EATING FOR THREE

"Mommy loves you so much," I said softly as I gazed at the two pairs of oval-shaped eyes staring back at me. I knelt in front of them, resting my knees on my bedroom's thick peach-colored carpeting. "You're the best babies in the whole world," I said, but they didn't react. They didn't move or make a sound, but I wasn't surprised. After all, they were Cabbage Patch Kids, and I was seven years old.

I had dreamed about being a mother ever since I had hopped out of my own stroller. I'd spent the early eighties tending to my dolls, lovingly changing their fake diapers and dressing them for school. I fed them and held them as though they were real. I called them by the type of names I imagined my babies—always daughters—would one day have, like Amanda and Victoria, names that made me think of beautiful girls with flowing hair and linen dresses, the type of girls everyone thought were so pretty. I had never had flowing hair or linen dresses, and I had never felt that pretty—but my children would. I baked fake homemade pies and cookies in my Easy-Bake oven and fed them to my dolls, confident in my parenting and sure that I was—and would one day be—the best mother. I was also the perfect wife to their daddy, played dutifully by my brother, as long as he did whatever I told him to do. My children, my husband, my life—it was all perfect in my childish head. I was sure that when I grew up, it would be perfect for real.

But I never thought that one day I'd go to war with my own body. I never thought I'd hate my reflection so thoroughly that I'd cut off its source of life. I never thought about all the ways spiraling into anorexia might destroy me or destroy my dreams. I thought only about being thin and how great life would feel when I was thin. But now, at thirty years old, as I sank deeper each day into a life of starvation, my dreams of motherhood were in conflict with my horrifying reality. Pregnancy would mean gaining weight—my biggest worry, the fear that dominated my life.

This wasn't vanity. This was *illness,* born from the loneliness and depression that had saturated my teenage years, leaving unclosed wounds that hadn't yet turned into scars. This was my brain's way of preventing a past filled with feelings of being unwanted and unwelcome from ever repeating. It was my mind's way of rewriting a story that was too painful to keep unfolding the way it had been. By the time I was twenty-nine years old, I had physically morphed into a different person, in a body that my distorted mind had convinced itself was worthier of love and attention.

Life for the previous four years had felt as though I'd been walking on a thin glass floor. Each pound threatened to crack the fragile surface beneath my feet. Gaining weight—any weight—threatened to send me crashing back into the place where I'd lived before, a world where I was invisible, unpopular, ugly. *How will this ever end? How long can I live without real food?* I loved being thin, I loved the way it felt to be called skinny, how my back would arch with pride and my chin would rise, and I'd pretend it was just the way my body was meant to be. I loved how my pants gaped at the waist, and I loved thinking that when people looked at me, they saw a woman with willpower and poise, so delicate she was breakable. But I hated everything about what it took to stay there. The endless calorie counting, the manic exercise, the anxiety, the control it had over my entire life: I hated every bit of it.

I knew that the upkeep was too much, that the hunger was unsustainable, that it couldn't be healthy to live like this, but I convinced myself that I was still okay. I thought I looked the same as every other slender woman walking around New York, skinny but not *that* skinny. *Being thin means giving up food,* I told myself. *Every thin woman is doing it, they just don't talk about it.* Denying how far I had deteriorated let me keep going. Denying how different I looked from everyone else allowed me to keep starving myself. I never said the word *anorexia,* not even in my head, even when I saw the new hairs on my back, even when people looked at me like they'd seen death. Anorexia wasn't far away, I thought, but I wasn't quite there yet. I wasn't *that* sick. I was still okay.

I knew that pregnancy meant doctors would be monitoring my weight, and I'd *have* to let it climb. I knew the doctors probably wouldn't let me just tell them my weight, or let me look away, like I always had before. After years of meticulously eating as little as possible, I knew I'd be forced to feed myself so my unborn children had nourishment. *How am I supposed to do that?* Eating for two was inconceivable when I couldn't even eat for one.

But I knew I'd have to if I wanted to carry a child, even if I had no idea how I was supposed to flip that switch. Pregnancy—in my distorted and panicked mind—meant choosing between the body I'd given up everything to have, and the life I'd always dreamed of living. Anorexia had taken away all the gray space when it came to weight. Everything now was a stark choice: emaciated or obese, happy or sad. Anorexia vaporized the middle ground. I wanted children more than anything in the world, and I wasn't willing to give that up. I wouldn't let anorexia steal that from me. *I just need to figure out how close I can get to safely doing both at the same time, and I need to get it over with as quickly as possible.*

"Let's have a baby," I said to Evan in March 2007, seven months after our wedding and just weeks after I'd come home from Mexico, stood on a scale, and wondered how thin you'd have to be to die. "Didn't we want to travel a little more before kids?" Evan asked, reminding me of the many conversations we'd had about enjoying married life together, and seeing the world together, before building a family. "We haven't really gone anywhere yet," he said. He was right, but I didn't want to go anywhere anyway. The thought of long trips, or any trips, had become too stressful. Along with romantic dinners and social events, Sunday brunches and holiday parties, anorexia had stolen traveling from us. Vacations meant too many restaurants to manage, too many hotel gyms to navigate, too many snacks to pack in case there was nothing I could eat. *What if I can't find food? What if the gym is closed? What if the restaurants won't change my meals?* There were so many what-ifs, and so much to worry about, that it drained the enjoyment from planning or taking any trip at all.

Evan and I had managed to take a trip to Israel around that time. In the tiny gym of our hotel, a woman in her fifties wouldn't get off of the only treadmill, even though I had made sure to sign up in the little notebook for the seven a.m. slot the night before. I got to the gym at 6:55 a.m. to find her walking fast on the machine, and once the clock hit the hour, I stood on the side, giving her a death glare. At 7:03, I walked up to the machine. "Hi, I signed up for seven," I said. She looked at me sideways and then looked away, continuing her speed walk. I stepped back and waited again, cursing her under my breath and counting the seconds, my stomach in knots. *The seven-thirty person is gonna show up and I won't be able to run and then I won't be able to eat and my day will be destroyed . . .*

Before I knew it, I had pulled the emergency stop cord on the treadmill. She stumbled backward off the machine. I climbed on immediately and started to run as she cursed at me. I ignored her until she left, running with my headphones on, hiking up the speed to make up for lost time, as I imagined her coming back with a knife or with her husband to kill me. I worried the entire trip about seeing her again or being arrested for assault in a foreign country. But I had to do what I had to do. *No one fucks with my workouts.*

So yeah: I was okay with not traveling. Plus, now that I was married, every time I saw a mom strolling her baby, I would get this feeling of longing. When I'd pass a store selling baby clothes and tiny shoes, I'd ask myself what I was waiting for. I loved the idea of finally having a real baby to care for. An actual baby to whom I could give all the things I had deprived myself of, like unconditional love, care, compassion—and food. "I don't want to wait," I told Evan, "just in case it doesn't happen quickly." He's just two years older than I am, and the thought of being a young dad appealed to him, so he didn't argue. "Let's do it," he said with a giant smile as he wrapped me in a hug and we held each other tight with excitement.

I was excited, but I was also really scared. Before Evan even stepped away from that hug, I worried about how I'd lose all the baby weight. With his arms still around me, I thought about whom I could ask for tips on dropping the pounds I'd gain from pregnancy. *Who's that woman everyone uses after they have kids? What kind of diet does she put them on? I wonder if I can lipo all of it off.* Despite the vortex of worry I was collapsing into, I also wondered if motherhood might save me. *Maybe once I actually have a baby, I won't care about being so thin. Maybe I won't have time to think about starving myself when I have to think about another life.* As much as I hated the thought of baby weight, and as confused as I was over how to get through a pregnancy, I couldn't have been more excited about being a mother.

But first my ravaged body would have to actually get pregnant.

A friend referred me to her obstetrician, Doctor A., and by the time I had my first appointment with him, after many months of futile attempts to conceive, I knew something was wrong. Doctor A. knew nothing about me other than what was in my charts, but I didn't want to cloud his judgment by asking the questions that ran interminably through my head: *Can this happen from not eating enough? Can this happen when you're too thin? Did I cause this myself?*

I didn't want him to think I was sick, so I'd let him draw his own conclusions. He was the doctor, not me.

Doctor A. said there could be several reasons why I was unable to conceive naturally, but I was pretty sure I knew what the reason was. The day Evan and I decided to try for a baby, I went off birth control in a flurry of excitement, but my period never came back. Month after month, I waited for my period, running eagerly to the bathroom at every imagined cramp, and nothing happened. Month after month, we tried for a baby, and nothing happened, because my body wasn't working the way it was supposed to. I wasn't menstruating or ovulating or doing any of the things a woman's body is supposed to do. The day after we embraced at the thought of having kids, I ran to a pharmacy and bought a stack of pregnancy tests so I'd have them on hand when I needed them. But the tests sat untouched in a bag under my bathroom sink. For six months, my body did absolutely nothing toward making a baby, and I knew it was from anorexia, even if I couldn't admit it to anyone else.

As I sat in Doctor A.'s office alone, staring at his plaques and diplomas through wet puffy eyes, I wished that I hadn't told Evan to go to work instead of coming with me. "It's fine," I told him, "don't miss a conference, I'm sure it's all routine and fine." But as I listened to my obstetrician run through the different causes of infertility, I didn't think it was fine anymore. I worried about all the ways I might have caused my body to destroy itself. "It could be fibroids, it could be issues with your thyroid," he explained as I sat in terror, playing out the worst-case scenarios in my head. "You'll get tested for everything." I didn't know if "everything" included eating disorders, because he never asked me any questions about food or weight, and looking back, I have no idea why. *He's not that kind of doctor,* I reasoned, relieved that I didn't have to discuss my eating habits with him. It was too late anyway, I was already broken. I didn't want someone to fix *me,* I just needed someone to fix the situation. I needed someone to find a way to get me pregnant.

As Doctor A. spoke, I imagined telling Evan he'd never be a father. I also imagined telling him that we'd need to adopt or use a surrogate, and that our dreams of lying in bed at night and singing to my pregnant belly, feeling our baby kick, and anxiously waiting for contractions to start would never happen. "It could also be Evan's sperm," he said, and I felt the weight lift a little. *What if this is all Evan's fault? What if I didn't cause any of this?* When I told Evan we'd need to test his sperm for problems, he seemed annoyed. "There's nothing wrong with my sperm," he said with a mix of frustration and cockiness, as if the thought alone was a threat to his manhood. But he was right. After he went to a clinic for testing, we learned there was nothing wrong with Evan's sperm. The reason I couldn't conceive was glaring, but no one would dare to say it out loud, not even the doctor.

I didn't know anything about fertility treatments, because I had no reason to know. My sister had gotten pregnant whenever she so much as looked at her husband, as had my mom, so I never thought I'd have a problem. But as it turns out, when you eat next to nothing and exercise way too much, as I had done for the past four years, there are repercussions. Anorexia can destroy your body in ways you might never imagine while you're busy admiring how an extra-small dress hangs on your figure in a dressing room mirror.

I'm not a doctor, but here's what I came to understand: starving your body of nutrition can interrupt the normal secretion of hormones from your brain, causing what's known as secondary amenorrhea, aka *no period*. In the simplest terms, *no period* means you won't ovulate, which means no baby—at least not without help. On top of that, my body fat was so shockingly low that my endocrine system was completely out of whack, so my reproductive hormones were all messed up, adding to the reasons I wasn't ovulating.

Long biology lesson short, my body knew I was in danger even if I refused to acknowledge that truth; my reproductive system had essentially shut down so my body could conserve energy to keep it alive. Even without knowing the exact science, I realized that I had single-handedly destroyed my chances of conceiving on my own, and I had no idea if technology could fix it. I didn't want to know whether I could fix it on my own by eating again and gaining a bunch of weight, because I wasn't ready for any of that. By then I was so deeply addicted to dieting and restricting that I physically and mentally could not stop. If I had known the truth—that recovery might make my body work again—I would have had to decide between my weight and my future, and I was afraid of what my decision would be. I didn't know if Evan and I would ever be able to have our own children, and it was my fault. All along, I imagined my eating disorder was hurting only me, that I was the only one who felt all the pain it caused. But now, for the first time since my spiral into starvation had begun, I felt like anorexia had actually caused tangible harm to someone else, someone I loved, not to mention the children I had always dreamed of having, and there was nothing I could do to reverse the damage.

"There's a great fertility clinic we work with here in the city," Doctor A. said. "But before we start with that, I want you to try gaining ten pounds and see if it helps." I looked away. If that was his way of telling me I was too thin, I didn't want to hear it. *If my weight was a serious problem, he'd have said it more seriously,* I reasoned. *He didn't say I had to gain weight for this to work, he just suggested I try.* But to me, that suggestion was the same as him saying "Just take a knife and try chopping off one of your fingertips." The feeling of terror when you imagine the act, the nauseating way your body seizes in worry when you can feel the pain that hasn't even happened yet—that's what I felt when he told me to try gaining weight.

Looking back, sometimes I wish Doctor A. had risked sounding like an asshole and given it to me straight. Sometimes I wish he would've stood up, walked over to the front of his desk and sat on the edge like a jerk, leaned over and looked dead in my eyes, and said, "Jackie, you're destroying your fucking life and your health; you're destroying your body, and you can die. You need to get help before you try to have kids." Maybe if he had done that, I would have hated him, and maybe I wouldn't have listened—but maybe I would have. But it doesn't matter, because all he did was lightly suggest I gain ten pounds. *Yeah, okay, Doc, sounds totally doable. I'll just go out and do that, be right back.* By now I was dying for a baby, but as terrifying as my prognosis was, I wasn't about to gain ten pounds when I had been presented another option. A fertility clinic seemed much more reasonable to me, and as anxious as I was about that process, it didn't match the anxiety I felt about gaining ten pounds out of nowhere.

But I *tried* to gain weight, as much as I could possibly try, which just meant I thought about gaining weight, and I tried to *rationalize* gaining weight. I looked at different foods in stores and thought about eating them. Sometimes I bought things in the hope that I could eat them, like little sandwiches in clear triangle-shaped boxes or single cheese sticks from convenience stores, just to end up throwing them away. Over the next two weeks, I gained one excruciating pound before begging my doctor to let me get started with intervention. "I can't gain weight, I've been trying," I told him in a frantic phone call when I couldn't bear the thought of pretending to try any longer. A few weeks later, I sat in the waiting room of a Manhattan fertility clinic for my first treatment.

"You should be fine. Don't worry," said the doctor I saw at the clinic, "stress isn't good for conceiving." He explained that he could medically help me create all the eggs that I couldn't create naturally, "and then we can see what happens, and if we need to try different treatments, we can do that." He was calm, unlike me, and he didn't mention my weight. That didn't surprise me at all, since doctors rarely mentioned my weight. Doctors mentioned my weight negatively only when I was fat, not when I was thin. Thin meant I ate carefully, I kept my body moving, and I wasn't at risk for heart disease or Type 2 diabetes or a stroke. I realized quickly that to most people, including doctors, weight is only a glaring issue if you're fat. Besides, I was sure this New York City fertility doctor had seen everything before. *He probably sees women half my size,* I told myself, *there's probably women much thinner than I am who come here.* By then I had relentless body dysmorphia, in which part of my brain knew I was the thinnest person in the room, but the other part saw most slender women as thinner than I was. "Am I thinner than her?" I'd ask Evan sometimes when a skinny woman would walk by. "You're half her size," he'd say with a sense of defeat but to my absolute delight. "You could gain twenty pounds and still be thinner than her." But even with my body dysmorphia, any time I looked around the fertility clinic's crowded waiting room, I knew deep down that nobody there was thinner than I was.

I trusted my fertility doctor, and he was sure something would work. For the first time in months, I could breathe again. *I haven't hurt Evan,* I thought, *everything will be okay.* The less invasive stuff, like Clomid pills to stimulate ovulation, didn't work. So we moved on quickly to in vitro fertilization (better known as IVF), where eggs are removed from the woman's ovaries, fertilized with a man's sperm in a lab to create an embryo (or multiple embryos), and placed back into the woman's uterus. *Thank God for IVF,* I kept saying in my head, *thank God I haven't hurt anyone.* As I prepared to stab myself with syringes full of medications, spend weeks swollen and bloated, and undergo surgical procedures to retrieve the viable eggs and implant the surviving embryos, I thanked the universe over and over that my eating disorder hadn't hurt anyone.

IVF is a godsend of modern medicine, but it doesn't come without a price, physically, emotionally, and monetarily. The monetary price is substantial, and we were fortunate that Evan's insurance covered a good percentage of our treatment. But the shots took a toll on my body and my mind. As my ovaries expanded from rapid stimulation, I felt swollen and distended. The hormones made me retain water, leaving me bloated and disgusted with how I looked. I was puffy, tired, and mentally exhausted, and I worried about the medicines having secret calories or making me gain weight. On top of that, the injections, which are meant to go into your fatty tissue, left ugly bruises. My anxiety was through the roof as I catastrophized everything. If this didn't work, I'd be letting everyone down, my husband wouldn't be a father, my parents wouldn't have any more grandkids, Evan's parents would blame me and probably hate me forever, and I'd be robbing my unborn children of a life and future.

I don't remember how many days I had to wait after the embryo transfer until I was allowed to take an at-home pregnancy test, but I remember counting down the seconds. On the day I could finally test, I peed on a stick and left it lying in the bathroom of our Manhattan apartment and walked out to meet Evan in the living room. "I have a bad feeling," I said. I didn't really have a bad feeling or a good one, but I needed to protect my heart and Evan's. The thought of starting over, the needles and pain, the endless clinic visits, the waiting and anticipation, of going through all of that again, was unthinkable. "If it doesn't work this time, we'll try again," said Evan, who was the best partner I could've asked for. But the truth is, no matter how amazing your partner is, a woman goes through IVF alone. You take the shots alone, you feel the physical pain alone, you fight your fears and demons alone, and if you have the misfortune to have most likely caused your own infertility, you feel the crushing guilt all alone, day and night and in your dreams.

Evan and I walked back into the bedroom together, and I turned to him one last time. "If it doesn't work, can we really try again?" I asked, to which he smiled and stroked my hair. "Of course. You know we can," he said. I knew, but I needed to hear it out loud one more time before I braced for disappointment. When I saw the two blue lines on the stick, I screamed so loud the neighbors could hear me. "I'm pregnant, I'm fucking pregnant!" I screeched to Evan as I jumped around our bedroom and we reveled in excitement. That night I fantasized. I thought about everything that was about to come. I thought about baby names and dieting, and room decor and which dieticians I'd call, and how we'd tell our parents and how I'd starve myself after I gave birth.

Though I had moments of pure joy, preparing for the life that lay ahead, I quickly discovered that being anorexic and pregnant at the same time is as horrible as it sounds.

"Just please tell me the minimum I have to eat to keep them healthy," I said somewhat frantically to the prenatal nutritionist I found through a friend. I knew I'd need to gain some weight during my pregnancy, especially once Doctor A. told me I was having twins and I'd have to come in regularly for monitoring and weigh-ins, but the thought of eating more food kept me awake at night. All the websites I checked said that the thinner you are, the more weight you have to gain for a healthy pregnancy, suggesting underweight women gain up to 55 pounds with twins, which made me feel sick from day one. Before I got pregnant, if I attempted to eat something that wasn't on my short list of allowed foods or didn't fit my caloric regimen, I physically couldn't eat it. It was as though my brain had a magnetic pole that matched the magnetic pole on food and auto-matically pushed it away, like when you play with repelling magnets as a kid. The ways I hated myself when I was overweight and the fears I had about becoming that person again, all of that would bear down and repel the food in an instant. But I had to figure out how to eat for my children, if only for a few months.

The nutritionist looked at me as though I were insane, but I didn't care. "You have to keep yourself healthy, too," she replied. "They'll need a strong mama once they're born." *Ugh, stop preaching, please, and just give me a fucking food chart,* I thought. *At least I'm here, someone really sick wouldn't even be here.* I reasoned that if I made sure I was eating *at least* the minimum amount we all needed right from the get-go, my babies would be fine, and that's all that mattered. "I'm super-healthy," I said. "I'm naturally thin, but I just want to make sure I get it right for them." The nutritionist gave me a standard list of nutrients with the ranges I should aim for when carrying twins, and I made sure to meet exactly the minimum levels for each and every one. I welcomed the pregnancy-induced nausea that made food seem grotesque, and I fought a manic compulsion to jog as I speed-walked on the treadmill. I battled the daily guilt that came from having empty foods like saltines to settle my queasiness, and that accompanied the extra calories I had to consume.

Late in my first trimester, I fainted in the supermarket. I hadn't eaten enough that day, and as I walked down the aisle, my head suddenly felt light and my vision got dark. I woke up with my back resting on a wall of canned soup, with other shoppers standing around me. The store manager crouched down and offered me a small bottle of juice while I called Evan and waited for him to come get me. "I'm okay, I don't want juice," I told the manager, repeating my stance despite his repeated attempts to help me. "I don't like juice," I insisted. I was so thirsty, and I needed something with nutrients, something with sugar, but I couldn't drink it. I looked at the little bottle, but I couldn't bring myself to take it, because juice went over my minimums. It should have been a wake-up call, but it wasn't. "Pregnant women faint sometimes," I told Evan. *Fainting is normal,* I told myself.

Some days I'd take walks with my friend Bella, who was a social worker in the maternity ward of a city hospital. Her job was to make sure new mothers were ready to leave with their babies, and sometimes she'd tell me stories about the people she'd see at work, while leaving out the confidential details. The stories I most wanted to hear were about the underweight moms, the ones who might've had eating disorders, although I never used those words. "Do you ever get people who don't gain weight when they're pregnant?" I'd ask, as if I were just curious and not worried that my body would give out before the babies came out. "Oh, we get women who are so tiny," Bella said, "they only gain what their babies weigh, and they're back to being so thin by the time they leave. It's sick." I pictured those women getting up the day after they gave birth, buttoning their skinny jeans, and taking their babies home, while I was sure I would be left with a floppy stomach and fat arms. It didn't seem fair. I wanted to ask if their babies were born healthy, but I didn't dare. I was afraid that if she said yes, I'd want to stop eating.

I never enjoyed being pregnant, but I found my groove early in the second trimester, once I understood how to eat for my babies without eating for me. Once I got to that place, where I felt like I had a system to keep my weight gain under control, my anxiety dissipated enough to let excitement set in. By the time the third trimester started, I couldn't wait to meet my living dolls. I wouldn't have to wait too long. Just before I reached thirty-four weeks, an ultrasound revealed that both babies had stopped growing, a warning sign that something wasn't right. "They have to come out. They'll grow better outside of you," my doctor said before sending me to the hospital for steroid injections in preparation for a C-section thirty-six hours later. I didn't ask if being underweight had anything to do with it, or if dieting during pregnancy contributed to their failure to grow. I didn't want to know because it didn't matter now. All that mattered was that my children come out with their lungs ready to breathe and cry and their bodies able to thrive. For thirty-six hours, until I heard those cries, I tortured myself with worry. I prayed that my compulsive dieting hadn't damaged my babies in ways that I could never undo. I had tried my best, but your best doesn't go far when you're that sick.

Jonas Mark and Adin Jett were born six weeks early, weighing under 4 pounds each, and quickly became the center of my world. I instantly separated my life into parts. There were the parts that involved my husband and children, that lit up my life from within. Every milestone brought me joy, every step filled me with pride, and being their mother gave me purpose. I took my babies everywhere, reveled in their smells and sounds, sank my nose into the folds of their necks and breathed them in endlessly. And there were the parts that involved food, that tormented me, that controlled my mind and body and drove me back into toxic habits with an intensity that I'd prayed wouldn't be there anymore by the time I gave birth. I'd thought gaining pregnancy weight would prepare me to let go of starvation, but it just made me desperate to go back to my old ways.

Jonas and Adin stayed in the hospital for nine days, premature but healthy, aside from their weight and some jaundice. The doctor called them "feeders and growers"—the exact opposite of the woman who had just birthed them—since they needed only to eat and grow before they could come home. But while my babies fed and grew, I starved and shrank. I had gained 43 pounds during pregnancy, which included the weight of my two newborns, and the number on the scale made me physically nauseated. Every time I looked at it, I vowed to get rid of every last ounce.

The way that some women miss wine or sushi when they're pregnant was the way I missed anorexia. The way they might dream of devouring steak tartare as soon they're done carrying a baby was the way I missed starving. I missed the safety of restricting and the emptiness that let me know I hadn't eaten too much. I missed the light-headed delirium of running on an empty stomach and the way skipping right over a meal made me feel like I had more willpower than anyone else. I missed the concave hollowness of my stomach. I missed all of it. Anorexia never left me during those seven months. It waited for me and quickly drew me back in. Within hours of giving birth, I went back to my old habits, eating empty foods with minimal calories. Within days I went back to my torturous workouts —despite the pain of my fresh C-section incisions—and within four months I had lost almost everything I'd gained. Almost: my new weight was 8 pounds higher than my pre-pregnancy weight. I couldn't get the scale to go lower no matter what I tried to do, but I was still very thin, easily a size 0, so I didn't mind.

Besides, being a few pounds heavier would keep people from asking questions or making judgments, I hoped. Not that anyone besides my parents ever questioned me to my face or judged me out loud, but I still didn't want people thinking that I might have a problem, because I didn't want anyone to pressure me to stop. I wasn't ready to stop. With a few extra pounds, people would think I was cured, that my eating disorder had magically gone away. Even my parents stopped making occasional comments and voicing their restrained worry.

I thought that once I had my body back, parenting would be relatively simple. Busy but simple. I was sure that once I could self-soothe with my toxic habits, I could handle whatever was thrown at me. But I didn't anticipate how hard it would be to feed my children when my own behavior around eating was so distorted.

I desperately wanted to breastfeed, but anorexia destroyed that, too. I frantically tried to give my babies breast milk, pumping my breasts day and night to give them everything my body could make, but you need to eat enough to have a healthy breast milk supply, and I was hardly eating after I gave birth. I was so set on restricting calories that I couldn't create enough milk to fill more than two bottles per baby each day. The mental battle to justify losing weight when it was costing me breast milk was too hard to keep fighting. After three months, I was pumping out next to nothing, and I had to give up.

Overall, feeding my infants was a mess, the exact opposite of how I had envisioned it. I had pictured my babies adorably breast-feeding and sucking down bottles of my milk as I cuddled them in my arms, then smacking their lips with delight as I fed them dinner. But that's not how it went. When my babies didn't want to eat, my behavior turned frantic. I'd spend hours trying to get them to drink a bottle, often locking myself in the bedroom so that no one would interfere with their feeding, pacing the halls of the apartment while trying to make them finish. Once they switched to solid food and started to resist eating, mealtimes turned into a frenzied sob-fest. I was so scared they wouldn't eat enough that I behaved manically around food. I never trusted my own hunger cues—when you always feel hungry, your hunger cues become meaningless—so I didn't trust theirs, either, forcing them to eat when they couldn't bear it, crying in the kitchen as my children sat in their high chairs craning their necks away from me so their mouths were inaccessible and knocking over their bowls of warm squash with their flailing arms and splashing thick orange puree on their white high chairs as I pulled my hair out and spun in circles day and night. "They won't eat," I shouted and sobbed to Evan night after night as our babies refused almost everything I gave them. Evan was always a calm to my turmoil, and when he took over, he seemed to get it done without any shouting or crying. Sometimes that got under my skin, and sometimes I'd tell myself that he probably just threw their food away when he thought they'd eaten enough, even if there was a lot left over; usually, though, I was so relieved to not be feeding anyone that I was thrilled to take a break from crying.

But when I was alone, I'd feed my children for hours so they would finish whatever amount a pamphlet or a website told me they should finish. I made faces and played with puppets, crying and wildly shaking tambourines, pretending to fall down so they'd open their mouths and take the food off the spoon. I was terrified that I'd be blamed if they didn't gain enough weight, because I was underweight myself. *She doesn't eat, that's why her children don't eat,* I imagined the pediatrician saying. *There's probably no food in the house,* I could picture people whispering. I thought everyone would accuse me of purposely not feeding my children because they could see that I didn't feed myself.

I used to wonder if motherhood might make me ease up on restricting or make me want to take care of myself more. Instead, it gave me an excuse to be worse to myself than ever. I used my children as justification to not nurture myself. I reasoned that my babies were an extension of me, and if I took care of them perfectly and made sure they grew big and strong, it was good enough for all of us. I reasoned that I just needed to worry about my kids.

The only way to make sure my kids ate enough, I thought, was to feed them *perfectly*, and feeding them perfectly required more than selecting the right jars at the store. The way I knew how to perfectly manage food was to micromanage it. And I had the time to micromanage their food—I was a full-time parent by then, having left my legal career halfway through my pregnancy, so I could be at home with my children. I started weighing all their food before I gave it to them, unless it came in a preportioned container that clearly showed me how much food and how many calories were inside. I insisted that they clean their plates, finishing every premeasured bite I offered them, no matter how many hours or tears it took. On the few occasions when I couldn't force them to eat, when my frustration level got so bad that I'd have to give up and throw their food away, I felt like a failure, and I worried that I was letting them starve. I scoured nutrition labels on the back of baby food cans and boxes to make sure they were getting enough nutrients. I kept track of their calories and how much meat they ate and how much milk they drank, with charts and papers stuffed into labeled binders, turning them into mini versions of myself to make sure I was feeding them enough, and hiding as much of it as possible from everyone, including Evan. I was tracking the food and calories of three different humans, and it was making me crazy—but I couldn't stop. I was so scared of underfeeding my children and so compelled to underfeed myself that my mind whipped back and forth between feeding and starving. The only way I could manage it all was by rigidly controlling every bite that any of us might eat.

When I wasn't struggling to feed them, Jonas and Adin filled my life with laughter and love and purpose. I compartmentalized the parts of motherhood that had to do with food, and the rest was everything I had always wanted. Giving up practicing law to be home with my kids was a decision I neither struggled with nor regretted; I was completely fulfilled with my role as a parent. The only part of my dream that was missing, though, was a daughter. The daughter of my imagination, with the long flowing hair and the linen dresses, the daughter who'd have a completely different life experience than the one I'd had. I really wanted to try for a daughter and have just one more pregnancy. Knowing what lay ahead for me, I wanted to get it done as fast as possible. I couldn't handle the anxiety over fertility treatments, the shots and bloating, the uncertainty over whether it would happen, the weight gain, the eating for two (or more), and the desperate race to be thin again. So when Jonas and Adin were a year old, just after we left New York City for the suburbs of New Jersey, I commuted back to the same Manhattan clinic to start another round of IVF.

The additional year of anorexia had ravaged my body even further. My estrogen levels were depleted, and my egg quality was awful. I did two more rounds of IVF and produced a few low-quality eggs. Each time the clinic called to tell me that none of the embryos had survived long enough to transfer into my body, I plunged into spates of darkness. "At this point, I'd think about the possibility of egg donors," my doctor said, "or maybe stopping altogether." But I was hysterical and determined to do as many rounds of treatment as I needed to get pregnant, no matter the gender of the baby. I couldn't let anorexia win; I couldn't let it cost me the family I wanted. I was determined to make it right, no matter how long it took or how badly it hurt.

I switched to Doctor M., a female fertility specialist in New Jersey who was willing to hold my hand and stick with me until I had a baby. "I don't care how many rounds it takes," I told her, and to judge by the way she smiled at me and nodded in agreement, neither did she. The next round of IVF left me with one embryo to transfer, and I was pregnant for a week before the little dot on the ultrasound screen disappeared, leaving me heartbroken. Despite the relentless bloating and endless needles, despite the brutal physical and emotional exhaustion of treatment coupled with caring for two babies at home, I kept going. Four weeks later, I started another round of injections. "You have two low-quality embryos," Doctor M. told me after my fifth round of IVF. "Let's put them both in and hope that one of them makes it." And so we did. When I went in a few weeks later for an ultrasound and saw two tiny dots on the screen, I nearly passed out in a delirium of happiness and terror. *Two sets of twins? Who the hell has two sets of twins?* By the time I found out I was having a boy and a girl, I was ecstatic and ready to get this last pregnancy over with.

I pulled out my old charts and food graphs so that I could once again eat the minimum amounts to have healthy children, but this pregnancy was riskier than the first. My daughter was hardly growing in utero, and nobody understood why. I didn't ask if it had anything to do with my diet, because I didn't know how to change. As long as I was eating the minimum that I had to eat, as long as I was doing whatever the doctors asked me to do, I absolved myself of responsibility for whatever happened. My doctor put me on modified bed rest at twenty-four weeks, which meant lying around without any exercise besides walking to and from the car at nursery school pickup. The blood in my legs wasn't circulating properly, so they'd turn a light shade of purple within seconds of standing up every morning. I hated my body, with its huge stomach and purple legs. I cursed it in the mirror, even though it was carrying the most precious cargo: the babies I'd spent a year stabbing myself with needles and crying for. I did nothing but worry, about my children, about my 40-pound weight gain, about how I'd lose all the grotesque bulges and lumps when the babies came out.

My second set of twins was also premature. At thirty-four weeks gestation, they completely stopped growing inside me, and my OB said they had to come out, which was fine with me. I had all the same fears and worries I'd had the first time around, but I was so disgusted with my body that I was relieved to be done with pregnancy forever. I just wanted to get back to dieting. I got another round of steroid injections to prepare their lungs for the outside world, and scheduled another C-section, this time in New Jersey. Hudson Matthew was my biggest baby, at just over 4 pounds, but Alexis Harlow was barely above 3 pounds at birth. They spent two weeks in the NICU, feeding and growing and overcoming minor issues, tiny but healthy, and thankfully better eaters than their older brothers. By the time they started solids, I was weighing and tracking their food as well. If anyone noticed all the tracking, I told them it was the only way for me to stay organized and make sure every child got everything they needed. And with four babies at once, no one second-guessed the way I kept order, including Evan, who was just grateful to have me in charge of all the nitty-gritty while he was at work.

"I don't know how you do it," people would say when they saw me strolling through Target with infants in a double stroller and two toddlers holding my hands. "It's organized chaos," I'd joke. "I just keep track of everything. Then I don't forget to do anything." Saying it out loud like that let me rationalize all the tracking, and no one could blame me for having a system to stay sane. But the truth was that I was now micromanaging what five people ate all day, every single day. My happiness depended on keeping the parts of my life separate. There were the food parts, where I'd obsess over numbers in a state of hyper-control, and there was all the rest, the parts where I didn't have to feed myself or anyone else, and I could experience incredible joy. But the food parts were incessant. Food was everywhere, and feedings were constant. Calories consumed my life.

I tried to hide the worst of it when other people were around, stashing the scales and the charts under cabinets, and trying to act normal around feeding time. I'm sure people noticed, like my in-laws and my mom. I'm sure they saw the scales and the charts, and sensed my anxiety when my children were eating, but no one knew what to say, so no one said anything at all. I acted like everything was fine so people would think everything was fine, but that also meant pushing away any feelings of guilt or shame about the things I was doing to myself.

Every once in a while, I'd get a tinge of sadness, a moment when I realized I was possibly missing out on life, but I'd let it go as quickly as it came. When my mother would visit the kids and tell them stories about when she was pregnant with me, I'd feel that moment of sadness. "When your mommy was in my belly, she'd kick me like crazy when I ate pizza," my mother would say with a laugh. My children loved those stories. "Mommy loved when I ate pizza, she stole it all away from me," she'd tell them. My kids would laugh, and they'd ask me if they ate up all of my pizza when they were in my belly. "Yes, babies, you ate all of Mommy's pizza. You left no pizza for me," I would joke, feigning anger over my stolen food. Usually, they'd ask what else they loved to steal from me when they were inside me, and sometimes I'd choke on regret. "Oh, you guys loved Doritos and burgers," I told them, "you stole all of my donuts, too." But I knew I hadn't eaten anything fun while I was pregnant. I didn't enjoy eating anything, and I hadn't eaten pizza or donuts or Doritos in years. I counted every calorie while I was pregnant, and controlled every bite I took, but my children didn't need to know that. They didn't need to know about any of it. I was determined to hide every part of my eating disorder from them. I told myself that my children were too young to notice my habits, even though they were literally always watching. I didn't hide the way I ate in their presence, because they were too young to know it was disordered. I didn't hide the way I restricted, because they were too young to know I was actually hungry, that I said no to things I actually wanted, that I was starving when I said I was full. They were watching, but they were too young to understand what was really going on. They didn't ask questions and I didn't offer explanations. They were just too young to know anything was wrong.

Having a family like mine was a built-in excuse for anything. "That's what happens when you have four kids under three," I'd say when I didn't want to go out to eat or attend a family event. I mean, who could argue with that? It was convenient for saying no to lunches and dinners or when I needed an excuse to skip a meal at home. No one could say I was exaggerating when I said I was too tired for dinner. "The babies need me," I'd claim, and run off before anyone could force me to eat. "I'm still trying to lose the baby weight," I'd say of my diet foods and workout regimen when I felt like I was being judged. "Exercise is the only time I get for myself," I'd say to justify my exhausting workouts. Taking care of my family and keeping my body thin felt like the only priorities in my life during those early years of motherhood. I told myself it was okay to neglect myself in favor of them. *That's what mothers do,* I'd whisper in my head. *We put ourselves last.*

Mommy's eating disorder was just another part of my kids' lives, and that's the way it was. They didn't know any better, so they came to see it as my normal way of being. My children didn't seem to care that I never ate the way they did, or the way other moms did, or the way their aunts and grandmas did. If we went out for ice cream, they knew that Mommy was just getting water, and they knew that if they raised their plastic spoon to offer me a bite with a look of pride on their little face, I'd respond with "Thank you, baby, I'm full." And they never complained.

If we went for pizza, they knew Mommy would just be watching them eat, sometimes sipping a diet soda, and if they lifted their slice with their tiny hands and said, "Mommy, do you want some?" I'd say something like "No, baby, I'm good." And they didn't seem to care.

They knew that Mommy ordered only coffee when we went to IHOP for breakfast, and that Mommy never wanted some of their snack, and that Mommy never had a bite of birthday cake on their birthday or on her own birthday. They knew that Mommy never shared their food at restaurants, never shared with Daddy, never ate at a backyard barbecue, never used salad dressing, never ate the bread, and never ordered dessert, but they didn't seem to care. Mommy didn't eat, and it just was what it was. As long as I saw my babies enjoying food, I usually didn't feel any guilt, and if I did feel guilt, I pushed it away. *My diet has nothing to do with theirs,* I told myself. *It's no one's business but my own. I'm not hurting anyone.*

I told myself that Evan didn't care anymore, either, that he had come to terms with who I was. If I believed that was the truth, that Evan didn't care about what I did or didn't eat, then I wouldn't feel guilt, and my eating disorder could keep going. *That's just me,* I thought, *he's giving me space to be me, just like I give him space to be himself.* Evan knew that if we snuggled on the couch and ordered in, he was ordering by himself. He knew that I'd never taste the dinner he cooked or let him surprise me with a meal. I'd never share a tasting menu with him; we'd never sample a delicacy on the streets of a foreign country together. He knew we would never take a culinary tour or do a whiskey tasting or share an appetizer or try new foods together anywhere. He knew his wife didn't eat, and it just was what it was. *My diet has nothing to do with Evan's,* I told myself. *It's no one's business but my own.*

I told myself I'd stop once *this* happened, once *that* happened. But in truth, nothing could stop me.

"Mommy loves you so much," I said to the two pairs of oval eyes staring back at me as I tucked my three-year-old boys into bed one night. "I would die for you," I whispered as I kissed their soft cheeks good night. Jonas's face turned visibly upset. "Mommy, don't die," he said, "I don't want you to die." I had never felt love like that, knowing you're someone's entire world. I smiled and leaned down closer to his little face. "Mommy's not dying, munchkin." I laughed. "It just means I love you. Mommy's not gonna die." Jonas touched my hair with his baby hand, playing with it between his fingers. "Promise?" he asked. "I promise," I said.

As I stood to leave their room that night, I felt the familiar emptiness of a barely filled stomach and the growing familiarity of a broken heart. As I walked into my bedroom, I felt the dizziness of hunger. As I lay down to go to sleep, I felt my ribs and my wrists, touched the bones of my shoulders, and ran my hands over my jutting hips to feel the rewards of my efforts, the rewards of starvation. And as I fell asleep, another day turned into night, and the night turned into another day, living in the hell of anorexia.

~❧~

CHAPTER SIX

DINNER AND A SHOW

On a summer morning in 2013, I took two small frozen containers of diet yogurt out of the freezer and placed them on the kitchen counter. Then I reached into the packed refrigerator and poured an ounce of skim milk into the tiny measuring cup that sat next to the toaster. I opened eight packets of Splenda, emptied four of them into my thermos of black coffee, added the ounce of skim milk, and poured two more packets of Splenda on top of each yogurt, slowly, as I scraped my way through my frozen breakfast. It tasted good enough, especially by the time I got to the second yogurt, which had melted just enough to let the Splenda dissolve slightly into the mushiness of the top layer of yogurt ice.

It had been ten years since I'd eaten a "normal" meal. Ten years with a full-blown eating disorder, a raging illness that I'd thought would last a few weeks, one that I had intended to be finished with when I got to a size 2 and I was sure that Evan loved me. An illness that I worked full-time to manage and to hide. I had gone through everything—a career, dating, marriage, pregnancy, motherhood, moving—all while hardly eating, rigidly controlling every bite of food, and compulsively overexercising. Every single day of those ten years, I had tracked every last bit of food that entered my body and every last drop of sweat that came off of it. I was the definition of a functioning anorexic.

I wasn't sad about my breakfast. I wasn't angry that I was eating like that or cursing into the air that I hated living this way. I hardly thought about my routine meals anymore. I was just happy that it was mealtime, so the emptiness could dissipate for a little while. This was my life. I derived my happiness from the parts outside of eating, and I had lost hope years ago that any of it could ever change.

I'd let go of any expectations of ever enjoying food and instead found fulfillment in other places. My children, my husband, the beginnings of a new career as a writer. I had found a rhythm in the way that I ate. I found safety in eating the same exact meals over and over, day after day, year after year. Food didn't matter, hunger didn't matter. When I was in college, a friend who didn't eat sweets would tell people that sweets "weren't her vice." I always envied that. She sounded so confident, so in control of her body and in touch with her desires, and back then, I wished that I didn't get so much pleasure from stuffing my face. Fast-forward seventeen years to when I had lunch out with a friend who watched me strip my garden salad of the croutons and cheese and sprinkle salt on top instead of dressing while I sucked down three Diet Cokes. She looked pityingly at my food. "That's the saddest salad I've ever seen," she said in a heartbroken voice, as if my salad truly made her sad. "I think it's great," I told her, trying to control my annoyance. "Garnishes aren't my vice."

After ten years of anorexia, when people asked if I wanted food, I'd smile and tell them that food wasn't my vice. Every day I grew increasingly numb to the idea of ever living without an eating disorder, because I had to be numb. I was so far gone, I believed there was no way out. The voices inside me that once screamed, that once prayed and begged for me to find a way out of this disease, were now faint, smothered in sickness, strangled by time. I could hardly hear them anymore.

Around March of that year, I'd started fighting with my mother. We had petty spats all the time, which were usually short-lived, but this time we were really fighting. My mother had found herself in the middle of one of the many conflicts between me and my sister, and after several months, it wasn't resolving. I was constantly agitated, and every day I grew increasingly stressed about it. I decided to find someone I could talk to professionally.

I found a therapist online who dealt with family trauma, and I made an appointment to visit her office in Manhattan. When I got to my first session, I found a tall brunette woman in her late fifties with expensive-looking glasses and a tucked-in button-down shirt. I looked at her flat stomach and lean legs and wondered what she ate for lunch to stay thin. We talked, but there was no spark between us, no moment of connection when I thought, *This woman gets me.* She listened to my issues with my mother, offered minimal feedback, and suggested another session to continue speaking. I booked another appointment, hopeful that we just needed to get in deeper, and the next week, I returned to her office. But a few minutes into our second meeting, I knew she wasn't the right fit for me. When our forty-five minutes were up, I thanked her and said I'd call her for the next appointment, which I had no intention of doing.

"Hang on, Jackie," she said as I turned to walk toward the door. "Before you leave, I want to ask you something." She paused. "Do you have issues with food?"

I froze. It was the first time someone had asked me that out loud instead of just staring at me and wondering about it in their head. *I'm not ready for this to happen. What is she gonna make me do?* "No," I said, furrowing my eyebrows to make it seem like she was so far off base that she should be embarrassed. "I'm fine." I smiled and turned again to leave.

"Wait," she said, taking a card from the top of her desk. It was her business card, with a name and number written on the back. "This is a dietician who specializes in treating eating disorders. You can do what you want with this, but please take it with you." The card had been waiting on her desk with the name and number written out before I came in for my appointment that day. Maybe she knew the signs of someone who starved herself—the mildly sunken cheeks, the bony arms, or the glazed-over look in the eyes. Maybe it was something I'd said during the session the week before, but I can't remember. I took the card and opened the door. "See you next week," I lied. *Stupid bitch.*

I got home and went straight to my bedroom, stuffing the card deep into my underwear drawer so nobody would find it. It was just a name—Leah—and a phone number, but it felt like a billboard with giant block print that announced, "Jackie's sick and she needs help and here's the lady who can help her!" I piled bras and socks on top of the card so no one would ever see it. Still, a fading piece of me held out hope that there was someone who could help me. I was afraid if I threw out her card, I'd be throwing away my only shot at recovery. I didn't feel ready to get better, but I was too scared to throw it out.

I thought about that card all night. *Maybe she can help me just a little,* I thought. *Maybe she can help me eat enough that I won't have to live with delirious hunger and complete deprivation anymore, but I can stay a size 0.* A part of me was terrified to even open the door a crack and let anyone see the way I'd been living, but I knew that no one could force me to recover if I didn't want to recover. *I won't let anyone make me get fat,* I told myself. *It's my life. I'm in charge.*

The next day I called Leah to ask what she typically did for patients who didn't have eating disorders but wanted to be less regimented. In other words, what she could do for *me,* since *I* didn't have the type of problems she usually saw. I knew that Leah couldn't force me to eat, or to tell the truth, or to follow any of her rules if I didn't want to, so I had nothing to lose by calling her. And I thought maybe she could help me just a little, just enough so I could get a touch better, so I didn't have to constantly starve and always tell lies, but not so much that I'd gain weight. I explained that I *did not* have an eating disorder, but that I followed a strict healthy diet, and I'd like to be able to add in more food without gaining more than two to three pounds. "I don't want to gain more than that," I said aggressively, almost like a warning. "Okay," she said gently, "we can talk about what you're comfortable with." "I'm comfortable with two pounds," I said. We made an appointment for me to come in.

I walked into her waiting room the following week and saw a girl sitting on the couch. She was sixteen or seventeen years old, and she looked how I'd looked on my wedding day, with skinny legs under her jean shorts and a gaunt but pretty face under her thin hair. Leah's office door opened, and the girl's mother walked out, touching her daughter's shoulder as they all said goodbye. I got suddenly and deeply scared. I didn't know what the hell I was doing there. *I'm not ready for this. I don't want to get fat. I can't go back to being fat.*

Still, I walked into Leah's office hoping that a dietician alone might be able to fix the broken parts of me that had allowed food to take over my life, that had allowed thin to become all I thought about. I hoped my dietician, in forty-five-minute weekly sessions, could give me a food plan that would work with the parts of me that were willing to sacrifice my health and happiness to finally feel noticed. I wanted dietary advice that would softly untangle my self-worth from what my body looked like to other people. I wanted my dietician to cure a mental illness. I don't remember our conversations verbatim, but I remember enough to know that they went something like this.

"I don't need a lot of help, but I'm probably a little too strict," I told Leah as I sat down in one of the two armchairs on the far side of her desk. I looked at the other chair and wondered if people usually came in pairs, if other people let their loved ones help them in a way that I could never bear to be helped. "There's just a lot of foods I won't eat because they're unhealthy," I explained calmly, "so I probably don't have enough variety. But I definitely eat." Leah took notes with a pen and paper as I spoke, nodding her understanding before looking up. "Okay, we can talk about how to add foods into your diet," she said. "First let's go through what you eat in an average day."

Recounting an average day was easy, since I ate the same thing almost every day. But I hesitated. "You can be honest with me here," she said. "It's the only way I can help you."

I wasn't ready to be honest, with her or with anyone. For a second I felt like crying. I felt like letting a flood of pain and emotion break through, defying the voices that kept me sick, so there'd be no turning back, so she'd know how messed up I really was and she'd see through the bullshit I was about to feed her. But the voices in my head were screaming for me not to do it, and they were too loud for me to think straight. *It's up to you, kid. You can throw it all away right now and get your big-girl clothes out of storage, or you can pull your shit together and stay the course.* "I really don't need *that* kind of help," I told her. "I just want more variety in my diet." I reiterated that any weight gain needed to absolutely stay at or under two pounds. *I'm in control here, not you.*

We went through a typical day of what I eat, and I was honest about the content, but I was omitting quite a bit. The full truth about the way I pushed and starved my body was too appalling for me to say out loud. I really did want to start eating more—*I mean, who doesn't?*—but it wasn't worth losing everything I had worked for. I hadn't run away from that life just to slowly start walking back.

"I have a few yogurts for breakfast, they're forty-five calories each," I told her. I didn't tell her that I dumped Equal or Splenda on top so they wouldn't taste like shit. "I eat six of them a day," I said. Actually, I ate ten a day, but that sounded like a red flag. I also didn't tell her that I froze them solid, let them melt slightly, and then scraped at them with a tiny spoon, obviously.

"I have a salad and a veggie burger for lunch," I told her. *Sounds pretty normal.* The salad was lettuce and fat-free dressing, and the veggie burger was made of soy and had 80 calories. I told her all of that, but I didn't mention that I used three bags of lettuce for lunch with a precisely measured tablespoon of fat-free dressing and two measured tablespoons of sugar-free ketchup on the side. *Red flags.*

My snacks were fiber snacks—almost all of them—because they had the lowest calories. "Like what?" she asked curiously. I answered, "Like fiber granola bars, fiber pitas, high-fiber chips, stuff like that." She asked if my stomach ever hurt. I told her it was fine, but that was an absolute lie. My stomach constantly hurt. I had incessant gas pains and cramps, and most days I was bloated and uncomfortable. When my stomach felt overextended with fiber, I hated being naked, even during intimacy. But I was scared that if Leah sensed anything close to a "medical issue," like maybe I was hurting my organs or something, she'd pressure me to stop eating my snacks. I thought about the two fiber bars in my bag. I always brought fiber bars with me in case I got stuck in traffic before I made it home for food. *You're not touching my fucking snacks.*

Dinner was fish and salad, I told her. "Every night?" she asked, and I squirmed in my seat. *Why is she asking like that, like in a judgmental voice? I bet the girl who was here before me doesn't even eat dinner.* I started to get annoyed with the questions. "I like to have Gorton's," I said when she asked how I cook my fish. She looked confused and said, "Gorton's, like the brand?"

"I buy it in the freezer section because I hate to cook, and they come in two-packs, and there's all different flavors and types of fish," I said, to make it sound somewhat normal that I defrosted a frozen block of fish every night. I told her that I chose two three-ounce pieces each night. One piece was always the 90-calorie grilled salmon, and the other was a choice of 70-calorie cod or 80-calorie flounder, and I would just throw it in the microwave. With an air of skepticism, Leah asked if I liked it. "I love it," I lied. "It's so easy to make, and I have four kids, so I need easy. And I just really like Gorton's."

As I said that, I thought about how ridiculous it sounded. With a whole universe of foods to choose from, dozens of varieties of fish and meats and flavors at my disposal, I expected this trained dietician to believe that I ate the same exact dinner night after night because I really loved Gorton's. If I hadn't been scared shitless, I might have laughed, and maybe then Leah would have started laughing, too, and we would have laughed so hard together that I could have finally started crying because the jig was up! I would have gotten caught in my own ridiculous lie. But that's not what happened. She just waited for me to go on. "My sides are a Wasa cracker and steamed spinach or mashed cauliflower," I added with a straight face. *But really, I don't have a problem. I don't need that kind of help.*

"Dessert is a pint of fat-free ice cream," I told her without giving details about the brand. "The whole pint?" she asked, slightly surprised. "Yeah, it's more like frozen yogurt," I said. "Sometimes I eat less, but it's pretty light, so I let myself indulge." Now, I didn't tell her this part, but I'm telling you because I want you to understand the truth about some of the things I willingly put into my body to feel some sense of normalcy and pleasure. Of all the terrible "foods" I ate in order to make hunger pains go away, or to feel some false sense of mild satisfaction, this one deserves a trophy. I mean, this fake-ass ice cream was the definition of bogus food. It was hands down the absolute crappiest-tasting "ice cream" you'd ever eaten in your life, I guarantee it. You could taste the chemicals on your tongue. You could feel the grains of phony substances in every bite. There was an aftertaste of whatever flavor it said on the container, like someone had tried really hard to keep the whole pint at 140 calories while still making it mildly flavorful and safely edible, but the rest went down like cold dirty water. And that was my indulgence.

But I would never tell Leah that, because she'd tell me to stop eating it. She'd ask me what I liked about it if it was so disgusting. She'd read off all the chemicals on the container if she knew how fake the ice cream was, then warn me about their side effects. Maybe she'd drown me in guilt as she listed all the healthier alternatives I could be eating, like a cup of cottage cheese with cinnamon or shit like that, and I'd have to lie and say I wouldn't eat the ice cream anymore when the truth was that I needed that fake ice cream. There were so few ultra-low-calorie foods I could eat, so few foods that let me close my eyes and pretend I was indulging. As disgusting as the fake crap was, I didn't want to stop eating it. It was the closest I'd come to real ice cream in years, and I didn't want to let that go.

"I also eat sugar-free gelatin with fat-free whipped cream," I told her, "five-calorie cups that come in four-packs." She looked at me like she'd heard that one before. "How many sugar-free gelatin cups do you eat a day?" she asked. "About six of them," I told her, but that was another lie. I ate twelve to fourteen cups of sugar-free gelatin a day, but I couldn't admit that because it was way too embarrassing. *Six isn't so bad. Nothing to see here.*

Leah asked if I use artificial sweetener. Yes, I told her, a lot. "Probably about twelve packets a day," I said, but that was one of my biggest lies. I used closer to thirty packets a day, on top of the gallons of diet soda I consumed. Artificial sweetener made my food taste good and made me feel like I was cheating the system. I poured artificial sweetener on everything. "Twelve is a lot," she said, "let's work on that also." *Sweet Jesus, can you imagine if I told her the truth? Her freakin' head would spin off.* I also told Leah that I lightly tracked my calories, but I didn't go into detail.

Leah wanted to talk about weight, and so did I, in order to tell her yet again that two pounds was all the weight I was willing to gain. I explained that when I looked good, I felt good, and when I looked bad, I felt like crap. Feeling good mattered more to me than indulging in heavy foods. She suggested starting slow, with one meal a week where I didn't count calories or restrict anything. My face got hot. *I don't know how to just do that. How do you expect me to just do that?* I instantly wrapped my right fingers around my left wrist, the way I always did when I got nervous about getting fat and needed reassurance that I was still thin. If my fingertips touched far away enough from my wrist bone, I knew my weight hadn't suddenly spiked. As soon as Leah said it, I instinctively wrapped my fingers around my wrist to make sure I was thin enough to even think about eating a meal like that. *Nothing's happened yet, you don't have to do this, just calm down.*

One dinner a week. It felt like peeking into the eye of a tornado, like sticking your little head right there over the edge of the funnel to see what it looks like inside, terrified you might get sucked into the storm.

"Sorry, but I think that might be too much," I said softly, try-ing not to seem panicked as numbers started shooting through my head. "That could easily add five hundred calories a week, and I'd gain a pound every seven weeks, which is seven pounds a year." But Leah didn't seem concerned. *Of course she's not concerned, it's not her life, it's not her body. She's not the one who'll have to deal with it when I put on seven pounds and none of my clothes fit anymore. I don't want to eat regular foods, I don't care about that, I don't even know what I'm doing here.* "One meal a week won't make a difference in your weight," she said. "Your body will know what to do with it."

But I didn't trust her, and I certainly didn't trust my body. My body had deceived me for years. It had never known what to do with food. I trusted calories, and I trusted math, not some stranger telling me that if I added a load of uncounted calories to my week, I wouldn't gain a load of weight. "I really need some kind of guidelines for doing this," I told her. "It feels a little out of control." So we figured out how much I should eat at this meal: half a salad plate full of appetizers, six ounces of meat, and one cup of sides. Leah said I should be flexible. "See how you feel at the meal, if you're more hungry or less hungry," she said, "and use this as a rough estimate." There was nothing rough about it for me; I'd live by these measurements. We called it a "freedom meal" because I was free to order new foods and free from counting calories during the meal. I made an appointment to come back the next week, hopefully to discuss having had my freedom meal.

Sitting down for my first freedom meal reminded me of an old movie that my mom used to love called *Moscow on the Hudson*. In the movie, Robin Williams plays a Russian musician who defects to the United States during a trip to New York. In my mom's favorite scene, Williams goes to a supermarket, expecting it to be like the Communist markets he's known all his life, and expecting to stand in a long line for the single type of coffee they offer. Instead, he's directed to a coffee aisle where he finds brand after brand of coffee, more coffee than he could ever imagine. Walking slowly through the aisle, reading the different coffee names and coffee types in awe, he's so overcome by variety and lost in choices that he cries, "Coffee, coffee, coffee," before collapsing in a state of total overwhelmed delirium. That's how I felt when, for the first time in ten years, I looked at a menu to figure out what to order.

The night of my first freedom meal, I sat in a plush chair in an Italian restaurant, ready to have dinner with Evan and another couple from our town, and nervously scanned the menu, top to bottom, over and over, trying not to pick the healthiest thing I could find. I was excited but I wasn't. I didn't want to order fish, because I'd instinctively count the calories and freak out over the oil, but I couldn't order beef because it was too indulgent. Lamb, pork, pasta, seafood, fried, sautéed, it was too much, and I suddenly didn't want any of it. I ordered chicken cacciatore, but I don't remember how it tasted. I just remember intensely trying not to count the calories. As I ate the food on my plate, each bite took me further away from being able to track the numbers, and my mind raced with worst-case scenarios. Voices screamed in my head as I ate: *This is going too far, Jackie, this isn't how it works. Calories in, calories out, that's how bodies work.* I weighed myself three times that week to make sure I wasn't abruptly packing on pounds, but the scale didn't budge.

When I saw Leah again, I knew I had to make it very clear that I couldn't add anything else right now. I had been overwhelmed by the meal. "I can't change anything or add anything new or do anything more right now," I said aggressively, my leg bouncing rapidly up and down. I was exhausted. *How do people do this? How do they eat without knowing how much they're eating?* I agreed to continue with one meal a week until I knew it wouldn't cause too much damage, worried that my body was storing all the weight gain and it would spill out in one fell swoop in a few weeks. I'm sure she would have liked me to continue adding nutritious foods and flexibility to my diet, but I had no interest in doing that yet. She agreed to leave things how they were, at least for the time being, because I had given her no other option. "So let's talk about what you feed your kids," she said.

I feed them like a champ, lady. You won't get anywhere with this. Do they have protein? Yes! Variety? Yes! Organic veggies? Yes! She asked if they were good eaters, and I said they were good sometimes, explaining that I'd often have to pull out all the stops to get them to finish a meal after they refused to continue eating. "Why is it important if they finish the meal?" she asked. "If your kids are telling you they're not hungry, why do you make them finish?" *Because how does a freakin' three-year-old know if they're not hungry, Leah? They need to eat, and that's my job, to make sure they eat.* After years of mechanical, ritualized meals, my connection between hunger and eating had been completely severed. I didn't eat when I was hungry, I ate when a paper said I was entitled to eat. I couldn't see the way my disorder was spilling over onto my children, and I never would have willingly hurt them or exposed them to toxic behaviors, but Leah could see what was happening. "So if you don't listen to what they're telling you about feeling full, how do you know when they've eaten enough?" she asked. Simple, I explained. "I count their calories."

Leah hadn't pushed me when I'd told her I wasn't sick, and she hadn't pressed me when I'd said I loved having packaged fish every night, but this was too problematic to dismiss. "Jackie, do you weigh their food?" she asked. I closed my eyes. "Yes," I admitted, overcome with embarrassment. "But it's only because I love them."

Firmly, but in a soft voice, Leah told me that I needed to stop weighing their food and counting their calories. "You need to teach your children that they can trust their own bodies," she said. "You don't want to pass these issues on to them. You don't want them to learn that they have to control food like that." Her words smacked me in the face harder than anything she could have said about my own health or about the way I treated my own body. I'd never loved myself the way I loved my kids. My job was to protect them and guide them, and instead I was taking them all down a dangerous path.

If Leah did anything for me, it was putting an end to the way I tracked my children's eating. I realized immediately what I was doing to my kids, how I was teaching them to eat, and how I was telling them they couldn't trust their own sense of hunger or fullness. I was setting them up for a lifetime of disordered eating. *Is it too late already?* I wondered. *Have they seen too much?* I was horrified by and so ashamed of my behavior—but only because of how it affected my children. I wasn't horrified enough to save myself.

I went home from that session and threw out every one of my food scales and never counted my children's calories again. As painful as it was, I didn't weigh any more of my own food, either. I knew that if the scales were there, I'd use them for my kids, so I packed up all five of them and threw them in the trash. I could still count calories without the scales, even if I was slightly off with my food amounts.

I had learned to estimate portion size almost exactly. I'd often test myself, slicing up things like tomatoes or turkey breast and guessing their weight before placing them on the scale to see how close I was. I was scared, but I knew I could figure out how to live without food scales. As small as it was in the massive canyon that was the depths of my eating disorder, throwing away my scales was at least something. Despite my fears of losing control and the safety I got from precisely measuring everything, I threw away my scales. I had lifted a finger to let go of the side of the pool, and I was proud of myself for that.

After a few weeks of one freedom meal a week, satisfied that my weight was safe, I added a second freedom meal to my week. Leah explained that my body needed the food and would know what to do with it. "Bodies are efficient," she explained, "you'll use the food how it needs to be used." I didn't completely trust her, of course, since I trusted only numbers, but she said that one additional meal a week wouldn't really make a difference, just as the first meal hadn't made a difference. "If I gain weight, can I go back down to one freedom meal?" I asked. "Yes, we can go back if you gain weight," she said. With that, I felt like I could try to add a second freedom meal to my week as long as I was hypervigilant about staying in control. I monitored my weight as though my career as a pro athlete or supermodel depended on every last half pound.

Despite the anxiety that came with the added food, I also had a glimmer of hope. I told myself that if the scale hardly budged, maybe I could keep making little changes and slowly find my way back to normal. If the scale didn't budge, maybe I could live a life where food didn't make me want to run in the other direction and starving didn't make me feel worthy. I gained less than a pound after three months of having two freedom meals a week, an amount I knew I could lose in an instant if I ran for a few extra hours one week. But instead of feeling like I had a handle on getting better and could move forward with my recovery, I found the opposite happening. I felt like I had pushed my luck as far as it could reasonably go. I felt like eating any-thing more would be greedy, gluttonous, and unnecessary. Two meals a week were more than enough. I didn't need or want anything extra.

It was more food than I'd had in a decade. It was two hours a week filled with new tastes and textures, limitless options, and in-credible flavors. There could be oil on my chicken and skin on my fish, and it was okay. I could share an appetizer that had cheese in it, and it was fine. I could finally relax and eat two entire meals a week without a world of worry. It was a gift that cost me almost nothing on the scale, a reward from the universe for all my sacrifice, and it was more than enough. *But you can't have it all, Jackie. The people who eat like this at every meal are fat, and they hate their bodies.*

And then I turned those two meals a week into a twisted game. I used them so I could fool people into thinking I was okay. I broke up the amounts I was allowed to eat, the half plate of appetizers and cup full of sides, and spread them over the entire week so I'd have three quarter cups of a side dish one night and use the other quarter cup to measure out eight tablespoons of treats, like hummus, at other points in the week. It felt like heaven. I was overwhelmed with choices. *Coffee, coffee, coffee.*

I made a spectacle of eating out. If I didn't have an audience, I ate Gorton's and didn't waste a performance. *Why would I waste a freedom meal if no one is watching?* But if people *were* watching? Well, I put on a show.

I made a fuss over menus, theatrically announcing to everyone that I couldn't decide between pork chops and steak! *You hear that? Anorexic chicks would never eat steak!* Anyone else want burrata? *See, I told you I'm fine, I eat burrata.* Can I try your polenta? *Would a sick person do that?* MMMMMM, ALL THIS FOOD IS SO GOOD! THAT FETA IS THE BEST FETA I'VE EVER HAD IN MY WHOLE FUCKING LIFE!

My loved ones seemed relieved to see me eating, especially Evan. I knew he worried about me. I could see it on his face every time I faked my way through a meal by pushing food around my plate, every time I ate lettuce out of a bag for lunch, every time I said no to whatever food item he offered. This was the most I was eating since the day I met him, and I knew he was hopeful that it was the first step toward recovery, not knowing the warped truth about the way I was manipulating those meals—and the people around me—as I ate. "I'm proud of you," he'd say as he happily scooped food from the shared appetizers we'd ordered, something we'd never done together. We'd never shared any meals, and now we were doing it twice a week. My parents were equally relieved, especially my mother, who always worried in silence about my weight. "Thank God you're eating now," she said, as though my disorder had disappeared and, ta-da, I was back to normal. "I can make you turkey meatballs next time I come over," she'd excitedly offer as I nodded, knowing I'd never touch them. I'm sure my friends noticed my new eating habits, too, but they never would have said anything either way. Even my closest friends knew that talking about my eating habits was off limits. On the rare occasions when the topic came up, I shut it down. I would turn away or aggressively lie about not being hungry or rant about being a picky eater. I never engaged in conversations about eating habits with my friends. I knew they'd give up eventually. I knew everyone would give up trying to change me eventually.

But while the dinner show was taking place, I was still nervously counting out portions in my head. *Is this six ounces? Or is it five? Was there a piece of meat hiding under the potatoes, or did I put it there when I was moving stuff around? Should I count the side dish as double because they used cream?* I found new ways to torture myself, intent on saving food for the week ahead, and leaving most meals hungry. There were new charts, new numbers to count, leftover portions, and unused appetizers. There was no room for bread or dessert, ever. My freedom meals gave me intense anxiety. At least with Gorton's, I could relax. At least I knew what I was eating, even if it was boring.

I spoke to Leah every few months over the next six years, and in all that time, the only other change I made was reducing my artificial sweetener to about twenty packets a day. I also cut out some diet soda, but everything else got worse. I started to compensate for my two meals a week by being extra-rigid the rest of the week, sometimes cutting pieces of food from my meal and throwing them away, overestimating my portion sizes so I didn't accidentally overeat, adding time to my workouts when I had the breath to keep going. My little spiral notebooks and Post-it notes still went everywhere with me. I had calorie-counting websites bookmarked in my phone browser so I could jump to them whenever I needed. Measuring spoons littered my kitchen, in every drawer, on every counter; they were everywhere, taking the place of my scales. I didn't eat anything without measuring spoons. I was a mess.

But fool people I did—at least I think I did. I even managed to fool myself. Sometimes I had the audacity to internally judge other women who didn't eat. Sometimes I did to them what people did to me just to see how it felt on the other side. "Do you want to even taste my lamb chops?" I'd ask my skinny friend who had taken two bites of her fish before putting down her fork, declaring herself full, and offering the rest of her meal to her husband. "That's all you're eating?" I'd ask in a concerned voice, knowing how much I hated when people did that to me. *Wow, she has serious problems,* I'd think, even though I was still skinner than she was. *I bet she doesn't even have any freedom meals at all.*

Leah tried, God knows, she tried. She made me lists of healthy, real foods to eat, lists that I folded and shoved into an unmarked manila envelope in my desk so no one would find them. She suggested alternatives to my regular meals and tried to help me figure out how to eat lunch in a restaurant, but nothing stuck. At one point early on, she asked if I'd like to speak to a therapist and offered to give me names, but I declined. My darkness gave way to light for two beautiful hours a week, and I could live on that. I told myself that I had it all, the freedom to eat when I needed to eat, and a size-0 body to go with it. I had it all.

If anyone was worried about my eating habits or my weight, they never said a word to me, especially now that I was a few pounds bigger after having kids and visibly eating right in front of them. Even the people who were trained to notice red flags said hardly a word. Doctors never made a big deal about my low resting heart rate, they just asked if I ran marathons. "Forty-three is pretty low, you must be a performance runner," they'd say. "Nope," I'd respond, "I just jog

on my treadmill." And then they'd move on. No mention of bradycardia, a condition indicated by an abnormally low heart rate (under
sixty beats per minute) in which substantial weight loss causes your
muscle mass to plummet everywhere, including in your heart muscle. There were no discussions about how this causes your heart to
become smaller and less efficient, causing a slowdown of the heart
muscle as your nervous system fights to conserve energy so the rest
of your body can function. No mention of how that can kill you.

No doctors mentioned hypothermia, either—where a lack of fat
cells causes the body to have such little insulation that you're freezing
all the time—as I wrapped myself in heavy jackets on warm days or
broke out in goose bumps when I had to remove my shirt for an ex-
amination. I never got on doctors' scales, ever, and no one ever argued
with me about it. I made up a weight that sounded okay, and despite
the bag of skin and bones sitting on their paper-covered table, doctors
never asked about the way I ate. My bloodwork showed a body so depleted of estrogen from my diminished reproductive hormones that
I was at high risk for bone loss and osteoporosis, but doctors never
asked if I had an eating disorder. My blood pressure was always low
from a heart that was struggling to operate with so little fuel, but no
one was too concerned. I wore a hormone patch at thirty-five years
old to counter the scarcity of estrogen, with no period and protruding
ribs, but doctors never asked about the way I ate. If my doctors were
okay with it, then hey, I was okay with it, too.

The weeks once again turned into months, which then turned into
years, and I remained anorexic. My children grew out of toddlerhood
and learned to feed themselves, but I never did. Life stayed the same.
I stayed the same, eating the same meals, running the same courses,

and tracking it all in the same notebook, day in and day out. I was okay with it because I was still numb. I compartmentalized my life. There were the parts of life I loved, and then there was food.

At the same time, in 2013, I set my sights on being a journalist. I had forever dreamed of being a writer. During law school, I used to study at a local Starbucks, and there was always a guy there who wrote for New York magazine. I'd watch him jealously, with his artsy black-framed glasses and flannels, as he paused in typing to consider his next words, as he listened to headphones and created content for the world to devour. I dreamed of doing that one day; I dreamed of being a journalist and telling people's stories. I hadn't worked since I was pregnant in 2007, and with my three- and five-year-olds now in school all day, I wanted to try to break into journalism, albeit with no writing credentials, journalism degree, or published samples to show for myself. I aggressively emailed editors, begging them to let me write for them, until one small editor at a tiny local newspaper said yes. I wrote him a parenting column, and he liked it, and he paid me to write it twice a month. That turned into one article at the paper's sister magazine, which turned into a steady freelance career with a bigger magazine, a weekly column in a major newspaper, and countless articles for *HuffPost, Scary Mommy, Good Housekeeping,* and other news sites. But every time I succeeded at something or reached a new writing goal, I was searching for the next accomplishment, for more and more external measures of success, worried that nothing I did was good enough. *You're a local journalist,* I'd tell myself. *You're better than this, there's more than this.* I wanted more, I wanted bigger. I wanted people to know my name.

And that's exactly what was about to happen.

CHAPTER SEVEN

HIDING IN PLAIN SIGHT

I'd been a journalist for five years by the time the casting agent's message came through via Facebook Messenger. I was a popular local writer with a steady part-time freelance career and a loyal following for my weekly parenting column, "Minivan Musings," which ran in New Jersey's *The Record* newspaper. But mostly, I was a mom, home with my kids, driving to and from sports, deciding what was for dinner, and moving laundry from the washer to the dryer. I sat in my minivan on a freezing night in January 2018, waiting for my son's basketball practice to end, cycling through my typical day, when the message from a casting agent appeared, asking if I'd speak to her about being on *The Real Housewives of New Jersey*. "I'm sorry," I replied, "I'm not interested," but I didn't want to hit send. The truth is, I was extremely interested—*I could finally have the big career I've dreamed of, this is everything I've wanted*—but I knew that Evan wouldn't be on board. At the time, we lived around the corner from a former Housewife, and every time Evan and I would pass her house and see the trucks and cameramen and producers and lights, we'd turn to each other and roll our eyes. "Who would do that?" he would ask. "Who would put their whole life on television?"

Well, it turns out, I would. A few hours after saying no, I wrote the agent back and set up a call, and then I asked Evan if I could take a shot at becoming a Real Housewife. "What're the chances you'll get it?" he asked. "One in a thousand," I told him, as seemingly half of my town was also vying to get on the show. With that, he shrugged and told me to go for it. The first call led to FaceTime interviews, where I answered questions as charmingly as I could, offering stories of my careers in law and writing, my fractured relationship with my sister, and my unique family structure of raising two sets of twins. I never thought the network would actually choose me, given how many people I was told were in the running, but I thought they liked me.

And I was right. The video interviews led to meetings, which led to test filming in my home to see how I'd do on camera, and before I knew it, I was getting a call in late March telling me that the role was mine. Soon after, I was standing in a dressing room at Saks Fifth Avenue surrounded by racks of clothing, trying to figure out what the hell I was supposed to wear for my new life on television.

Evan wasn't quite as excited as I was. "I'm happy for you, but I don't want to do this," he told me one night in the kitchen, a few days before filming was to start. "You can do it," he said, "it's just not for me." I started sobbing and told him I needed him to do it also. "New Jersey is about families, please just try," I cried. "I can't do it without you. I won't let anything bad happen to you." I never asked anyone for favors, and it made me uncomfortable to beg anyone to fulfill my needs, even my own husband, but I *really* wanted this. I was too close now, and I couldn't turn away. "I bet you'll end up loving it," I told him. "Evan, I've stayed home for ten years while you've built a career. I need to do something else." So he agreed to try, and with that, I catapulted our lives into the public domain. I had no idea what to expect, but I couldn't wait to get started.

had been a Housewife for three weeks the night I sat at a table in Oklahoma for dinner with my new castmates. So far, I liked everyone, even though I instantly got closest to Melissa, and I was already close to Margaret. All of the women had such a handle on how to be a Housewife, how to offer staunch opinions and start interesting conversations, how to wear loud clothing and put giant waves in long hair. Even the other new Housewife, Jennifer, wasn't afraid to go big right from the start, basically telling the hostess that the sunset from her home in New Jersey was better than the one we were all admiring there in Oklahoma. It was the first group dinner of my first cast trip, and I decided that night to lie to everyone and say I'd recovered from an eating disorder. I didn't feel bad about misleading them—I hardly knew these women and would never trust them with sensitive information—so when I saw an opening to get ahead of anyone noticing my bizarre behavior around food, I pounced. Anyway, I thought it would make for good TV, overcoming sickness and recovering from trauma. I knew there was a risk that someone would call my bluff and point out that I hadn't eaten anything on the plane or at the airport on the way over. But I was pretty sure that wouldn't happen, not after the heartwarming story I was about to offer.

I still wasn't sure what the hell I was doing or what I should be doing as a reality star, or whether my outfit of plain skinny jeans and a crewneck sweater was too boring for the glamourous show I was on. Maybe I should've added something furry, like Margaret's fancy fur collar, or put elaborate curls in my hair, like Teresa and Dolores. My pants felt tight, so as the others spoke, I lowered my hands under the table and circled my fingers around my left wrist, to make sure I was still thin.

Coming to dinner that night, I had no idea what the hired chefs might serve, but I had a plan, the way I always did when I was stepping into a situation that was out of my control. I always had a plan. Since I organized my food and calorie allowances into weekly units, I had saved tonight for one of my two weekly freedom meals—the same meals I had started eating five years earlier, in 2013—which meant it was one of two meals each week where I didn't count calories, just portions. The meal portions were exactly the same: I could have up to six ounces of any meat I wanted, half a salad plate of appetizers, and an entire cup of sides, enough to fool anyone and keep myself somewhat full. I loved those nights, even though I usually relived the whole meal in my head that night and the next morning to make sure there had been no oversights, like extra sauce on the meat or a mistake in my calculations. I lived one meal at a time, and at least for this meal, I was safe.

Since Margaret had planned the trip to Oklahoma, we were joined for dinner by her business manager, Lexi, and Margaret's friend Polly, who owned the stylish country home where we stayed. The eight of us, six Housewives included, sat at a wooden table in Polly's farmhouse-chic kitchen. Rustic walls of natural stone and iron hanging pots surrounded state-of-the-art appliances, while an outfitted trailer sat outside the back living room windows. The food came out, individually portioned for each of us. A piece of steak, two sides of potatoes, and bacon-wrapped asparagus. Not the lightest meal, but at least it wasn't breaded or fried, which would've meant I'd have to scrape the breading off the meat before I could eat it, which would've looked really bad. The women talked in turns, and as they spoke, my focus flipped from worries over what might be served to my strategy for how to eat what was in front of me. I knew what I was working with, so my brain started to do the math.

In my mind, I portioned the massive square of steak on my plate into one-ounce pieces to figure out where I'd need to stop eating, and I mentally marked the location where my six-ounce meat allowance ended, using a specific spot of sauce as a marker. In my head, I tackled the potatoes, mentally dividing them into four quarter-cup portions. I wouldn't touch the asparagus. *Even if I move the bacon off with my fork, it'll have bacon debris that I'd have to count as meat.* My meal was now safe, even if I would feel guilty about the steak later. I also had a Ziploc bag full of portion-controlled Fiber One snacks in my suitcase upstairs if I needed more food at night. I never traveled without my fiber snacks, so I knew that I could always eat *something,* even if I had to skip all of my actual meals. Within seconds, I had figured out my plan of action and was able to flip back to the conversation at the table.

Teresa, one of the other Housewives, described the strict diet she was following as she trained for a bodybuilding competition, noting her rolling cooler bag filled with grilled chicken and broccoli. I studied her plate as she talked, flashing back to all the times I had sneaked my own food into restaurants so I didn't have to lose sleep about overeating something that *might* have been prepared with oil or butter. I'd hide my bony hands under the table as I slowly removed the small package from my bag and unwrapped tinfoil from a piece of microwaved fish to subtly add to my plate.

Teresa wasn't eating the steak or potatoes; she was eating a piece of grilled chicken with a plateful of steamed vegetables and was damn proud of her discipline. She wasn't hiding anything—in fact, she was showing off her plastic container of broccoli to the table. The chefs warmed the food she stored in the refrigerator and brought it to her seat with no backstory or explanation needed. I would've broken into a cold sweat and made up a thousand excuses if I'd needed to eat my own food, but Teresa didn't give a shit; she was just doing what she needed to do to win the competition. She declared that this was what she needed to eat to be at her leanest, and everyone seemed to admire her dedication. *Thank God,* I thought. *If someone else is acting crazy around food and getting away with it, no one will care what the hell I'm eating or not eating.*

But I knew her crazy couldn't compare to mine because her rules were temporary; the day her contest was over, she'd probably go for a burger and a margarita and not even think twice. I stared jealously at her steamed broccoli and wondered what I would eat if my diet were ever over. *Maybe a burger and a milkshake or some pizza or a big bag of Swedish fish.* I let myself daydream for a second about a day that I knew would never come. I'd never be free from my self-imposed rules and restrictions around food. I once again flipped back to the conversation at the table.

Teresa was still talking about her diet. She offered her plain broccoli to the table as Margaret laughed and told her it was a good thing she'd brought her own food. "Otherwise, you wouldn't be eating anything," she joked. *Is this my chance to get ahead of anyone picking up on how I act around food? Am I really doing this?* If could explain my behavior before they noticed, they'd think nothing of it, if they ever did notice, right? I decided to go for it.

"I had a pretty bad eating disorder," I said, and began launching into stories from the darkest days of my anorexia, when eating any food without a reliable nutrition label felt like jumping into a spiraling abyss of weight gain and loneliness. The steak on my plate was partially eaten, as were the potatoes, the perfect setup to convince everyone that I didn't have any problems anymore.

When I was going through the casting process, I'd had no intention of mentioning my eating issues—past or current—to anyone. After having kids and settling in a few pounds heavier, I felt like nobody questioned my weight anymore. And now that I could publicly eat normal food twice a week, I could "prove" that I was fine. I knew how to hide my eating disorder. I felt like I could control the narrative on camera the same way I'd been controlling it in my real life for the past five years, since the two freedom meals had come into my life. Maybe someone would think I was a tad too disciplined, or maybe they'd think I could stand to gain a few pounds, but I was sure the women at the table knew nothing about eating disorders. I was actually pretty sure that no one in the room knew anything about eating disorders, because for fifteen years I had felt so incredibly alone, like I was the only woman suffering while the rest of the world ate pizza at leisure and fluctuated on the scale without doing sprints for the rest of the day. No one else had to starve themselves to be thin; they were just thin, or they weren't and didn't care, and I was the only person I knew living in this much physical and mental pain around food. So how would anyone ever understand what I was going through? Truth is, there are millions of people who silently suffer with eating disorders, and thousands of people who die every year from anorexia, because almost no one talks about it publicly. But I didn't know that back then. It wasn't glamorous to admit how much work it took to stay thin, it was just glamorous to *be* thin.

I figured the women at the table would probably think that people with anorexia would never eat steak and potatoes. *How can you be someone who doesn't eat if you eat steak and potatoes?* It wouldn't make sense, so they'd assume I was telling the truth about my anorexia being in the past. Only I would know that I was lying, which was fine. Besides, I was thin, but I wasn't *danger-zone* thin like I once was, when my spine shouted through my clothing, "LOOK HOW EMACIATED I AM," and I had to wear winter jackets in the warmth of late spring to cover my shivering arms. I wasn't thin the way I was before I had kids, even though I tried desperately to get back to that size. My weight just wouldn't go any lower no matter how malnourished I was, no matter how I starved myself outside of those two meals a week. I had learned to live a few pounds heavier, a size 0 instead of 00, and had come to terms with it years ago when I realized that it threw people off my scent. People expect anorexics to be emaciated, and I was just really thin, so I could fool everyone, even myself. I convinced myself that if I were danger-zone sick, people would notice. I convinced myself that plenty of healthy women were a size 0 in their forties.

I had never spoken to Evan, my closest friends, or any loved ones about my eating disorder because they were too close to me, and they'd know this crap about recovery wasn't my truth. They could see the ways I still avoided food, how I measured and obsessed over every bite, how eating terrified me, and if I started a conversation about my "past" habits, they might challenge my dishonesty and try to force me to recover. But no one at this table—or on social media—knew how I behaved when cameras weren't rolling. They would take me at my word, so I could tell any story I wanted. And that's just what I did.

While the cameras rolled, I told the women stories about bringing my food to restaurants and obsessing over food scales, and how I'd weigh every single thing I was about to eat before I felt comfortable eating it. "When I first had kids, I started doing that to my kids' food," I told their astonished faces, "and I was seeing a nutritionist, and she said, *You stop it right now.*" I said it proudly, as though it were my aha moment, even though I knew my aha moment had yet to come. "I think that was the beginning of really knowing that if any of this might rub off on my children . . . I said, 'Forget it, I'm finished.'"

The women at the table were all proud of me. "Good for you," they all said. "I had no idea," said Melissa. "That's amazing," added Margaret. They were proud of me for overcoming such a hard time in my life. I told them that was how I'd stopped starving myself and

how my eating disorder had ended. And everything was true except
for the parts about how I'd stopped starving myself and my eating
disorder had ended.

I immediately worried that if I ever told the truth—the whole
sickening truth—about what I was still doing to myself, they'd
shame me into recovery, and everything I had spent so long starving for, the thin beautiful body I'd earned, would be gone. What
if someone said on TV that my children would suffer or that I was
killing myself and then I still didn't stop? I'd look like a fucking
monster.

*If I can make them think I'm coming clean from the start, they'll
just think that any strange eating patterns are scars of old wounds, and
I'm just a careful eater.* I knew deep down that anyone who looked
long enough or hard enough would see I was still sick—still so very
sick—but at this point, I was sure I could find a way to cover it
all up. I needed to control the narrative, but I didn't consider that
opening the door might make them look harder down the line instead of taking my word for it and looking away forever.

The hostess brought out a homemade dessert, and luckily, I had
skipped one of the quarter-cup portions of potatoes, so I could take
four tablespoon-size bites of banana pudding: the perfect end to my
story. So perfect that I had to call attention to it. "It's a fucking test," I
said with a laugh, a big exclamation point on the end of my grandiose
lie. "She's like, 'Jackie, let's see if that eating disorder is still here,'" I
joked as the whole table laughed and Polly happily scooped banana
pudding onto my plate. As I dug into the first of the four tablespoons
of dessert that I was allowed to eat, my brain was screaming what I

hoped everyone else could hear loud and clear through their TVs and into their consciousness for as long as I'd be on this show: "I'M EAT-ING DESSERT! NOTHING ELSE TO SEE HERE!"

What I didn't know then but quickly learned was that no one really ate much during filmed meals. First of all, no one wants to talk with a mouthful of food, and no one wants to get caught with food in their teeth or risk dripping sauce on their shirt and having to fin-ish the scene looking like a slob. Eating doesn't look as glamorous as having a few small bites and sipping wine. And I soon realized that if I procrastinated taking a bite for just long enough, a heated conver-sation or screaming fight would probably explode, and no one would give a shit how much of my Cobb salad I'd actually ingested.

Still, I was shocked by how good it felt to say the words out loud—"I had an eating disorder"—even if I was guilty of the sin of omission in how exceptionally present this fucking monster was every second of every day in my current life. Anyone who really knew me, who saw me for more than the occasional meal, knew I was struggling. I told myself that nobody knew about my eating disorder, that even my husband knew almost nothing, but it was impossible not to see. So I never talked about food in any capacity with anyone except the dieticians I'd seen along the way. It felt good to put even a fragment of my story into the world, so people could tell me how far I'd come and how strong I was, and maybe if I heard that enough, I could convince myself that I was strong enough to stop starving myself. Maybe if the entire cast and the audience of viewers and all of social media could tell me how great I was for getting past my eating disorder, I'd find a way to actually get past it.

I was given an idea of the shooting schedule, which allowed me to always make a food plan ahead of time. Some scenes would be meals, but lots of scenes didn't center around food, like shopping scenes or group activities. Most important, it turned out that no cameras would be left at my house when I wasn't filming. That was my biggest fear, because there's no way I'd be able to hide my eating habits if I were always being watched. Knowing that I wasn't going to be constantly monitored, I could strategize about how to manage my eating. I could ration my calories to fit the filming schedule, so no one would notice a thing. By the time filming started, I had developed a system for working out and eating that would get me through the entire filming season. I wrote out every rule on a blank page in my food diary, with bullet-pointed details about numbers and measurements, exchanges and tricks, and underlined and aster-isked reminders of the most important rules.

300 minutes of cardio/week plus 700 sit-ups, 350 push-ups divided over as many days as needed;

**2 meals per week of ½ plate veggie-based appetizer, 1 cup side dish, and 6 oz. meat. Divide meals as needed per week to accommodate filmed meals.

Safe foods on camera:

Lunch: grilled chicken (35 cal/ounce grilled), grilled shrimp (25 cal/ounce); salad w/ no dressing. Lettuce = 10 cal/cup or 15/cup shredded. Cherry tomatoes = 3 cal each.

Snacks = medium apples (100 cal), pretzels (6 cal per mini), crudites, grapes (4 cal/grape).

I'd keep a running log of my weekly cardio minutes, so if a cast trip meant skipping two or three days of exercise, I could make up for it before I left. Compensation was my saving grace.

But the thrill of starting my new life as a reality star was at war with the constant worry of having to eat something on camera outside of my rules. The fear of losing control of when and where I had to eat made me even more regulated at home. I'd make little changes that I knew would add up, like cutting my meals by a third and using salt instead of dressing on salads. I had to prepare for times when someone would cook something special and I'd feel expected to take a bite, or times when I'd be served food with a weird sauce or butter on it. I hated sauce, and I didn't care what anything tasted like anyway: when you're anorexic, taste doesn't really matter. All that matters is having access to food that you feel safe eating. You just need to replace the sensation of starving with the sensation of being full, and it doesn't matter if it tastes like crap. That's probably better, because you won't actually want to keep eating it.

By the time I was halfway into filming my first season, I already loved being a part of the show. It opened a world of new experiences outside of being a stay-at-home mom, expanded my friend group enormously, and gave me a new career I never thought I'd have. My concern about eating on camera had largely dissipated because I felt like I had a handle on faking my way through meal scenes. When the show came on the air, I realized that most viewers didn't notice our food consumption, focusing on the drama, not how much we were eating. It was easy for me to fake it. When Margaret hosted a spa day at her house midseason with an omelet-making station, I loaded my plate with an omelet, bread, and fruit, cut up the omelet, moved the bread, ate the fruit, got in a fight, and then we all left the table in disgust. Rinse. Repeat.

During my first season, my eating disorder was not an issue, because everyone took me at my word that my issues were in the past. I didn't look the way anorexic women are portrayed on television, all frail and emaciated, and I knew I could use that to my advantage when I first got on the show. Plus, plenty of Housewives were really thin, and nobody seemed to really question their weight. Once I made my eating disorder old news, everyone stopped paying attention to what I was or wasn't eating. And I intended to keep it that way.

But while I had a handle on the group meals, it was the smaller scenes that threw me. I didn't know how to eat between meals without knowing the calories of my food, so being offered something like a pastry was a nightmare. If I had to eat it, I'd use up almost a quarter of what I was allowed to eat all day, and not knowing exactly what was in it would send me down an hours-long dark hole of googling and worry. *Was there extra cream in the middle? Extra jelly? Did I underestimate the size?* Pastries are the extreme example, but anything I couldn't control—even milk—made me crazy, and I had to find ways to compensate.

Later in my first season, when I met Teresa at a coffee shop to hash out our issues, I panicked. Teresa was upset because earlier, when she'd told Melissa that a wife can control her husband's behavior, I'd told Teresa that *her* husband wouldn't be in jail if she could control his behavior. I thought we could fight and make up, like the other women always did, but Teresa hated me from that day on. I had love/hate relationships with almost everyone else on the cast, and I had good times and laughs with everyone else. But there were no good times with Teresa after that, there was no love/hate, only her hating me.

However, going into that meeting, her feelings were at the bottom of my list of concerns. My only concern was the coffee and how I'd order it in a way that didn't hint at any problems. *What if they sweeten my coffee without me asking? I need to say unsweetened, even if it looks a little crazy, because some places sweeten their iced coffee. And I always put the milk in myself, even if it's behind the counter, because they might use cream by mistake, but that sounds crazy, and I can't do it on camera. People don't understand how little milk I want.*

My plan was to ask if they had skim milk—a reasonable request—and ask for "just a drop." "Drop" was a safe word because there was no way they'd give me more than an ounce if I requested a drop, and I wasn't asking to pour it myself, so I felt okay with that.

When the episode aired, people read into my order. As a new public figure, I couldn't resist knowing what people thought of me. The thrill of fame made it impossible for me not to look at what people on social media said about me, even when it was bad. Comments were slowly starting to appear on recaps of the episode. *She won't even put milk in her coffee. She doesn't even use sugar. She still obviously has problems.* At that point, the comments were few and far between, and while my castmates never mentioned them, I noticed them. I worried that a producer would pick up on them, but I also took them as a sick compliment. *If they think I still have problems, that means I'm skinny.*

By the spring of 2019, filming my second season on the show, I found that it wasn't as easy to hide all my disordered behaviors and rules from my castmates. People were starting to catch me at off times, during non-meal scenes, where food would casually be offered, and everyone would eat except me. Unbeknownst to me, my castmates were increasingly noticing that I'd never touch a piece of bread or casually accept a treat if I went to someone's home. I never ate dessert, indulged in a random snack, or used dressing on my salad. I called it discipline and gave all the right excuses for not eating, but I didn't know they were about to start calling my bluff.

In May 2019, we took a cast trip to Jamaica, where I shared a suite with Margaret, my closest friend and ally on the cast. I had known Margaret before I joined the show, having been introduced by a mutual friend a few years earlier, but we only became close when I started filming in 2018. By 2019, she was one of my best friends despite my being ten years younger. Margaret was confident and outspoken but also a kind and caring woman, and she was definitely braver than I. I'm sure she never got a pit in her stomach when she was about to fight with someone, or overthought every comment people made behind her back, like I always did. As far as TV Housewives go, she was a great role model for me.

Our suite was all the way across the resort property from the rest of the Housewives, all four of whom were staying together in a duplex suite with a giant living room and pool. As we walked into our suite for the first time, my eyes darted to the dining table full of food. *Shit. How can I get away with not eating any of it?* I was rattled. There was fruit, but I couldn't always eat *just* fruit; it was suspicious to always go for the lightest thing on the table when there was so much more to eat, and I knew that. I felt trapped in a confined space with thousands of calories. My plan was to avoid being near the table until we could leave for our dinner scene.

Once we settled in, Margaret wanted to discuss what might happen at dinner that night. At this point in the season, half the cast, including Dolores, Teresa, and Jennifer, had decided that I didn't fit in with the rest of the group, based on various factors like having a nanny growing up while my parents worked, and my policy of asking family to call before coming over rather than walking in unannounced. They used those bits to declare that I had different values and was "cut from a different cloth." I was already on edge going into dinner because I knew several Housewives would be attacking me, making me feel like an outcast. When Margaret sat down at the dining table, I took a seat across from her and tried to hide my panic over the food. *Please don't ask me to eat.*

While some of my castmates seemed to have body-image issues (judging by the number of surgical procedures constantly being done to their bodies), Margaret had the good fortune of being able to eat what she wanted when she wanted, intuitively knowing when to stop, and never shaming herself or hating the way she looked. She enjoyed food in a way I never have and never could. During our conversation, she was eating sushi from the platter the hotel had left us. Mid-conversation, she offered me sushi. *Fuck, Margaret, don't do that to me, please don't make me say no on camera.* I hated being put on the spot or told to eat when I didn't want to eat. "I'm good, we're having dinner in two hours," I said. "And your point is?" she jokingly asked. I didn't respond, and I didn't take any sushi, I just moved on to a different subject.

Later in the Jamaica trip, I had an outdoor lunch with Melissa. She has been blessed by the heavens with the single most incredible metabolism I've ever witnessed in a person outside of my son Jonas, who consumes Nutella by the bucket and remains a human string bean. Melissa ordered a pizza and chicken wings for us to share. I ordered salad and a glass of sparkling rosé because I knew the calories in every bite and every sip. I could hold a full conversation while keeping a running tab of my intake and not skip a beat. But there was no room in the plan for pizza or wings. I didn't even want the dishes in front of me. I hated when people ordered food for me, when they took control of what I should be eating and took that control away from me. "I'm not really that hungry, I just wanted a drink," I announced, to take any expectations off what I might (or might not) eat. That way, if she asked why I wasn't having any pizza, I could remind her that I'd already said I wasn't hungry.

Melissa and I talked about the other women, and as she spoke, I thought about how many calories it might be if I took two bites of something to appease the audience, before I chickened out. I leaned back in my chair, as though sitting in the sunshine with a good friend and a glass of wine were heaven on earth, when, actually, being expected to share a pizza and wings made it feel like being in hell. But Melissa didn't say a word about the lettuce I had for lunch, and I thought I'd made it through our meal unscathed.

I often caught myself watching my castmates eat during meals, watching them casually take bread and butter, order mixed cocktails, and eat dinner without stopping to overthink everything. I was so far away from being like that, from not worrying about every bite and what it would do to my body and my peace of mind. So counting calories was my safety net—the only way I could eat without worrying that I'd suddenly gain a massive amount of weight—especially while starring on the show. No matter how many filmed dinners they scheduled or how much food I ate, as long as I counted the calories and compensated for overdoing any given meal, I could keep everything running smoothly. But when your sense of safety revolves around counting calories, eating breakfast on camera is a nightmare in a way that other meals aren't.

Whenever we were filmed eating breakfast, someone—usually Melissa—would fry a load of bacon and eggs and fill the table with excesses like sliced avocado and buttered toast. You might not get a table of fried foods for breakfast in some other cities, but no one's afraid of some olive oil and fried pork in New Jersey! No one, it seemed, except me. Everyone would casually eat as they were talking while I went down a dark hole of anxiety. If there was fruit on the table, I would fill my plate with berries and a few other foods I had no intention of touching, and I'd move the other foods around while I ate only the fruit. If there wasn't fruit, I was stuck. I'd panic and declare that I wasn't hungry. "I'll just have coffee for now," I'd announce in a singsong voice. *Lah-de-da, everything's fabulous! I'm just not hungry at all!* But I was always hungry, and breakfast scenes left me keenly aware of how very disordered I was. I couldn't eat any of their food if I tried, no matter how hungry I ever was.

Before cast trips, the production team would ask for our food and drink requests, and I'd always strategize around my dietary restrictions, requesting fruit and light yogurt for the refrigerator so I could seem to casually grab some berries or yogurt at breakfast to eat alongside everyone else. According to my logic, it didn't matter what

I had for breakfast, since everyone would have seen me eat at dinner the night before and therefore wouldn't second-guess my behavior.

But on the first morning of our cast trip to the Hamptons, weeks after Jamaica, I didn't see any of my fruit or yogurt in the refrigerator as the breakfast scene unfolded, and as a mess of greasy foods filled the dining table, I panicked, realizing there was nothing I could eat. "I'm not like super-starving, I just want coffee," I said to avoid any questions about why I wasn't eating. Then I saw a bag of quinoa chips on the kitchen counter, and having seen the nutrition label the night before, I knew they were light enough to eat a few without ruining my day, so I started eating those instead. "I want these chips," I said as Margaret stared at me in disbelief. "They're so good," I added as everyone else ate the food on the table. I never would have done that had I known my eating habits were being dissected, but I still had no idea anyone was watching me like that. If I'd known, I would have eaten some avocado and obsessed over calories later, escaping to my room to google the nutritional value of avocado and calculate the damage. Or maybe I would've had coffee and nothing else and said my stomach hurt from dinner. Eating quinoa chips at nine a.m. while a full breakfast was available was a much bigger red flag than eating nothing. Plenty of people only want to sip coffee first thing in the morning, but if you're hungry enough for food and an entire table of freshly cooked breakfast is available, reaching for a bag of dehydrated plant-seed snacks is a warning sign to anyone paying attention.

None of my castmates said anything about it at breakfast, but when the show aired, there was a scene where Margaret and Jennifer shopped in town before lunch. Jennifer told Margaret I was

cheap for having only pizza at my sons' birthday party, and Margaret stressed that the lack of food wasn't about the money but instead
about the way I viewed food. "This morning we're all eating eggs
and avocado toast, this, that, and the other thing, and she's eating
chips out of a bag," Margaret said. "Food doesn't even occur to her."

Just after that, the entire cast met in town for lunch at a popular Mexican spot. The night before, I had saved a portion of my
freedom meal for the lunch scene that I knew was coming, so I had
a few ounces of meat and a half-cup of sides I could apportion to
lunch; since I knew that tortilla chips were around 15 calories each, I
could also have five chips without doing much damage. And thank
God for that, because it was all I had to fall back on when the moment I had been dreading all along suddenly happened.

"Margaret said you have issues with food," Jennifer shot off with
a shit-eating grin and not a single care that she had just shattered my
carefully crafted world. Of course, she meant that I *still* had issues
with food, as opposed to the recovery bullshit I had slung to the
women over a year before in Oklahoma, a story I was sure everyone
had bought. Margaret could see through my lies and excuses, and
in true Housewife fashion, instead of bringing her concerns directly
to me, she'd brought them to another woman—Jennifer—who I
felt was always happy to knock me down. "She's the one who made
jokes about you not eating," Jennifer added. My eyes welled as the
two women launched into a debate over what Margaret had actually
said and why she'd said it, as the realization of what I had to explain
away surged through my shoulders and down my back.

By the grace of God, another fight erupted before I could say
more than a few words. It's the type of deflection you pray for when

you're the one in the hot seat. It doesn't happen that often, especially not during juicy conversations, but it's the type of interruption that takes all eyes off you and centers them on somebody else in an instant. After Jennifer had thrown utensils and salsa at Melissa over a comment about the way we raise our kids and half of the table had left, I knew that I could explain away their concerns about my health, and my eating habits could continue. The women who'd walked out were the only ones who might've continued second-guessing me. *I have to clean this up. The world has to think that I'm fine.*

I sat back down with Margaret and Melissa, my only real friends on the cast, to explain any "misconceptions" about the way I ate. I needed to tell more stories, and fast, so I could shut it all down again. Before I could get my words out, Margaret pointed out what had become obvious to everyone around me. "I say this because I love you, but I do notice you don't eat," she said. (When the episode aired, flashbacks captured multiple times when I'd turned down food.) Sometimes I wish Margaret had brought her concerns to me off-camera, so I could've avoided the fiasco I now faced, but I know that's not what we're paid to do. We're paid to have these conversations in front of the world. "What are you talking about, don't say that," I cried. I was in a cold sweat. *Keep your cool, Jackie, you've got this, and you have the half-eaten lunch in front of you to prove your points. Now do what you do best and shut it down.*

"I don't understand," I continued, gesturing wildly over the chips and spilled salsas that littered the table. "I just ate a whole thing of chips, a whole plate of guacamole, and drank two beers before my lunch came out." I was trying to keep my composure, but inside I was terrified. "Don't say I don't eat." *Please don't say I don't eat, please just take me at my word and let this scene be over.*

I started to tell stories. I told them about how far I had come since the days when I didn't eat, and how I'd put myself into treatment and saved my own life. I told stories about my trip to Mexico after my wedding, how I'd eaten nothing but canned tuna the entire trip, "and I came home and got on the scale," I said as I wept through my words, "and that day, I was like, I'm gonna die, and I was like, I just gotta help myself, because I'm gonna die." Margaret and Melissa were speechless, like they had realized that they'd gotten it so wrong—I really wasn't sick anymore, and it was all a terrible jump to judgment on their parts—and didn't know what to say. I kept going: "And I went and got help, because I came from a place where I really didn't eat."

Margaret grabbed my hand as Melissa wrapped her arms around me. I felt bad lying to them when they clearly cared about me, but I had to protect myself. "I feel horrible," Margaret said as tears streamed down my beet-red face. "I'm in such a heathy place," I declared, "so don't say that I don't eat." *I worked too hard for this and suffered too much for this, and these fucking women aren't taking it from me.* "The place I'm at now is just so good," I insisted, "that when I hear people set me back and take it all away from me, it fucking kills me." *Let's see them open their mouths now.*

At the time, I was sure they bought it. I thought I had shut the conversation down and explained it all away with the proof on a plate in front of me. Thank God I had saved a half-cup allowance of guacamole from the night before.

In retrospect, that fight over whether or not I ate was the best thing that could've happened to an anorexic who was hell-bent on secretly maintaining her anorexia. They'd caught me at a time when I *was* actually eating, and I'd had a story ready to go. Maybe I looked like someone who watched her diet, but I didn't look like someone with a real problem, whose food issues were worth a storyline. And with that, no one seemed to talk about the way I was eating anymore, at least not to my face.

By the time I got to the next season, I was basically a pro, used to the drama, the hectic schedule, and social media dissecting every part of my life. But while being on a reality show definitely has its perks, it can also be wildly unpredictable.

Plenty of people I knew watched *RHONJ*—and loved it—for the crazy fighting and over-the-top stories, but even if you didn't watch the show, most people I encountered knew what it was all about. Maybe you knew a friend of the woman who'd gone to jail or a neighbor of the one who'd had her extensions ripped out at a country club, but none of your friends were actually on the show. People constantly warned me that it could get dirty. In the same breath as they reveled in my excitement, people close to me cautioned me about the potential pitfalls. But I'd gotten through two seasons of petty fights and name-calling without any real trauma, even with the attempts to expose my sickness, and the thrill of celebrity was still new and exciting. I felt good about continuing, and I was sure I knew how to play the game. Aside from my eating disorder, there were no secrets I was keeping.

As it turns out, though, you can't stop people from placing skeletons in your closet, even if none truly exist. And you can't stop people from starting rumors, even when they're the type of rumors that could destroy your marriage, your family, and your life. I couldn't predict what was about to happen as I started my third season on the show. But as my life descended into chaos, I took comfort in dangerous old habits, and I could feel myself slipping away.

CHAPTER EIGHT

❧

THE BEGINNING OF THE END

When it comes to his birthday, Evan is a simple man. He wants heartfelt cards, a day off from work, and a vat of his mom's homemade gazpacho followed by angel food cake. What he's never wanted is a party, and since I've known him, he's never had one.

"Just this once," I told him, sharing my plan to kick off Season 11 with the first cast event—a party to celebrate his forty-sixth birthday. "Can you please pick something else to celebrate?" he asked, even though he knew he'd probably lose this battle. Hosting the first cast event held prestige, and this season, I wanted it. I rented the outdoor space of a pretty Greek restaurant, one that I knew Evan loved. "You'll have a blast," I said. "We'll also invite our other friends, and I promise to keep it low-key." Despite his reluctance, Evan agreed to be the man of the hour for just one night. "You'll have so much fun, baby, I promise," I told him.

As far as I knew, I was right. Everyone there had a great time, drinking and toasting after months spent locked down in our homes. It was August 2020, and no one had really gone anywhere since March, when Covid-19 hit the scene, forcing the whole world to socially distance and canceling almost every social event in its path. Covid had made my anorexia even worse. Sitting home with my immediate family, I had no one to impress with my food consumption. I rarely ate things just to show my kids I was eating, because I didn't think they noticed or cared, and I figured Evan had grown numb to my habits already, so I cut my freedom meals down to once a week and spent extra time on my treadmill since there was nowhere else to go. The thought of being trapped at home with a full fridge and a stocked pantry made me so nervous about eating past my caloric limits that I filled up on lettuce whenever I got hungry outside of mealtime. I wasn't trying to lose weight in the early months of Covid, I was just trying not to gain weight. Nonethless, I was secretly disappointed that my extra efforts didn't make the scale budge.

Now there was a reason to start leaving the house again. Filming for Season 11 had finally started, and here we all were, on the night before Evan's birthday (as he wanted to spend his actual birthday with our kids), with everyone in a celebratory mood. I hoped I would get some interesting gossip in the morning when I recapped everything with the girls, as we often did after all-cast events.

Once everyone left the party, I went to settle the balance with the manager, who asked if everything was okay.

"There was a fight in the bathroom," he said.

"Are you sure?" I asked.

No one mentioned anything to me. I would have heard about it.

The next morning, on Evan's birthday, my cell phone rang bright and early. It was a close friend who had been at the party, so I answered on the first ring, excited to hear what she thought about meeting the other Housewives.

She didn't sound excited.

"Are you alone?" she asked. "You won't like what I'm about to tell you."

I felt sick before she even started speaking. She told me that Teresa had spent the evening telling everyone on the cast and their significant others that Evan was cheating on me when he went to the gym. Most of their reactions were confused looks that asked, *Are we really doing this to Jackie?* They knew it was probably a lie, but Teresa must have figured it would cause an explosion, and she didn't care where the shrapnel landed.

As my friend spoke, I went dark. My husband's family is his entire world, and he values few things more than his reputation as a father, a spouse, and a stand-up man. He's never cared to be famous or the center of attention. Little things in life make him the happiest. Over two years earlier, I had begged Evan to let me be on this show. I had promised him nothing like this would ever happen. "No one will try to hurt *you*," I'd assured him. "The show is about the wives." I hadn't been lying to him, as I'd never imagined something like this would happen.

I called Margaret in hysterics, not because I couldn't handle a fight but because I knew it would kill Evan to have his name destroyed in front of the world.

"Listen to me—do *not* make it a big deal," Margaret warned me, urging me instead to put it to rest, since I knew it was a lie. "Tell Teresa she's fucking jealous," Margaret suggested, "and then let it go away. Don't tell Evan anything yet," she said, "because it'll blow up."

I'd always valued Margaret's advice, but I had to tell Evan before I continued filming. I couldn't let his name be viciously thrown around and his reputation trashed while he remained ignorant for the sake of my job. I couldn't let this storyline about his character play out while I fought it out on television and he unwittingly waited at home only to find out after the fact. It wasn't my name, and as I saw it, it wasn't my place to decide what to do. I would do whatever he wanted me to do, even though I assumed that he'd ask me to leave the show. I would tell him everything, but for the rest of that day, I held my tongue so he could at least enjoy his birthday. I was about to ruin the rest of his summer.

Before that birthday party, I had spent almost two decades using food to manage situations that felt out of control. Before Evan's birthday, life had felt steady, and though anorexia was with me every day, it didn't scream in my head endlessly at all hours. It was just there, quietly directing my routines, while I carried on as usual.

Now my husband would have to defend himself in front of his family, his parents, his colleagues, and basically *the entire fucking world* because of ME. It didn't matter that it was a lie, or that I didn't believe it, or that friends told me no one else would believe it, because I knew there *were* many people who would believe that my husband was a fucking slimeball who was cheating on his wife and kids. All I could think was how angry he'd be and how much he'd hate me for doing this to him. *Will he blame me? Will his parents hate me? What will I do with my life?* It hadn't been even a day since the party, and I was reeling. I could feel my thoughts pulling me into a bleak space. I'd already lost any desire to eat.

The next afternoon, I walked onto our patio, where Evan was finishing a call. I sat across from him as he rubbed my leg and smiled before putting his phone down and lifting his face to the sun.

"Hi, baby," he said. "It's beautiful out."

If I'm calm and act like it's nothing, maybe he won't lose his mind. Evan knew the way the show worked. The women had fights, we talked about people behind their backs, we embarrassed each other a bit, then we'd generally make up and move on. Sometimes the husbands got involved, but usually just as a sounding board. Evan had filmed a lot during our second season and was known for being a handsome, devoted dad and close friend to the other husbands on the cast. He was never the drunkest or the loudest, he never started fights or had huge moments of his own. He was enjoying the show, for the most part. Even my kids enjoyed the show, filming occasional scenes, getting in their cute one-liners, and attending Housewife parties on camera. I typically gave them the option of saying no when they were asked to film, and my kids almost always said yes. When it came to the show, we had all settled in nicely, to my enormous relief. Evan was happy, the kids were happy, and so was I. Until now.

"Can I talk to you?" I asked.

"Of course," he said gently, but he knew something was off. I never started conversations like that. Evan and I had faced it all—health scares, job crises, parenting emergencies—in our seventeen years together, but this felt like a new kind of serious. I was always sure we could get through the other stuff together, but I didn't know how this would play out.

I told him everything I knew, everything I'd been told, and said I didn't believe anyone had known in advance that Teresa would do this, but also that it couldn't be stopped from playing out now that she had. Evan was silent for a moment.

And then he went fucking nuts. I mean, like, FUCKING NUTS. "I knew this shit would happen," he screamed. "I told you this shit would happen. This fucking show, it's this fucking show." His face was all red as he shot up out of his seat and gripped the back of a patio chair with both hands.

He asked me a thousand questions I couldn't answer, as my heart sank and he yelled into the air. I told him all that mattered to me was what he needed.

"I'll leave the show if that's what you need. I'll never film again," I cried. I apologized over and over, but that wasn't what he needed. What he needed was for his name to be cleared.

Now, Lord knows I tried. In fact, anyone watching Season 11 of *The Real Housewives of New Jersey* knows I tried. I asked Teresa to sit down with me at Margaret's house (since that was neutral territory), and I explained to her the pain that her rumor was causing my husband and the damage it could do to my family—to my children—but she was unmoved. She'd never liked me, and I'd never cared, but I thought that after coming face-to-face, mother to mother, she'd understand my position and would admit that she had nothing to back up what she'd said.

She gave me nothing and started doubling down. In an attempt to explain to her the immensity of the pain this was causing us,

I made an analogy, equating the rumor she was spreading about Evan to someone saying that her adult child snorted coke. The mere mention of her daughter's name sent Teresa into a blind rage: she ran hysterically from Margaret's house, screaming, "Your fucking husband's cheating on you!" and calling me a c-nt no fewer than six times. I wasn't face-to-face with her again for over a month of filming, during which time the rumor was the center of endless cast-member discussions.

When we finally came together at Dolores's Jersey Shore house and I attempted to make peace, another explosive fight broke out when Teresa accused Margaret's husband of having heard the rumor as well. "Why are you pushing it, Teresa?" said an exasperated Margaret, aware of how much damage Teresa had already done. Margaret and I were both amazed at how easily she could continue to try to hurt someone she knew was hanging by a thread. "This girl's about to start crying again," shouted Melissa at Teresa, "it's her marriage." But Teresa didn't care, pointing her finger at me and calling me calculated, telling me she only liked confident people. "I'm a confident person, you're so not," she said. "I like hanging out with confident people." *What am I doing here?* I thought as I wondered how Evan would react when he found out he was still the center of the discussion. *Why did I even come here?* I was on fire. I hated Teresa so much in that moment, I felt like throwing the fucking platter of spaghetti all over her fucking head. But I couldn't do that. Instead, I brought up the thing I knew would sting the most—her time behind bars. "Did you get that confidence in jail?" I asked. Her response was as nasty and vicious as you'd expect, and she left the scene calling me every name in the book.

Now, people do *not* want to see the same fight drag on and on, so after about six weeks of fighting, during which Teresa continued to imply that my husband was fucking around, she offered Evan and me a cheap apology after being pushed into it by Dolores and (Melissa's husband and Teresa's brother) Joe Gorga. "Listen, Jackie, I'm not trying to hurt you in any way, you or your family, so can we just drop everything?" she said as we stood on Melissa's beach house deck in the early afternoon, not even a day since she'd once again tried to humiliate me over dinner, reiterating her theories about Evan and eviscerating me until I'd left the table in tears. When Evan arrived moments later to Melissa's house, Teresa offered just as lame an apology: "Sorry about, like, everything that went down," she said, "I never want to do anything to hurt you guys in any way." Missing was the part about having no evidence to back up the bullshit reputation-smearing story she'd told in front of the world, but at that point, we had no emotion left to give the fight and no tears left to waste on anything Teresa Giudice might say. We accepted her half-assed apology in order to end the story and get her off my back, and we coexisted for the rest of the season. But when the show came on the air a few months later, a social media battle erupted.

The season opened with Teresa spreading the rumor, of course, and her explosive reaction to my analogy. Over the next several weeks, as viewers watched the rumor take hold and the cast gossip endlessly about my husband's alleged cheating, people went wild online with vicious opinions about my marriage, my husband, and me. People salivated over the drama and spent several days after each episode having forceful debates over who should be believed: Team

Jackie or Team Teresa. Although plenty of people voiced support for us, the masses of Teresa fans came for blood.

My husband and I were often tagged in vile social media posts. There were countless Instagram messages and Twitter rants; there were Reddit boards devoted to Evan's cheating and degrading comments on pictures of my family about the women my husband was supposedly screwing.

I know his girlfriend, she's a trainer at his gym.

He's a f*cking cheater, Jackie, just look at his eyes.

Jackie's too ugly for him—that's why he's banging other women.

He's f*cking your sister!

At least now he's getting head.

After they hit send, they went back to their normal lives. But my normal life was stuck in a new reality, swirling around inside a fabricated story. For me, it felt like the season was about how much of a beating I could take, how much humiliation my husband could endure, and whether my marriage would survive. With every new headline or podcast or YouTube video that emerged about his supposed cheating, Evan grew more embarrassed and more enraged, and there was nothing I could do about any of it. I frantically called people trying to get things removed from social media, but any victory was a Band-Aid on a bullet hole. The stories and the comments kept coming, and if Evan and I tried to talk about any of it, we'd fight. For the first time in our marriage, there was an unbreakable and obvious tension between us. Enough so that our daughter was terrified we'd get divorced. Enough so that neither Evan nor I slept peacefully for months on end.

Even though Teresa and I had "reconciled" while filming, we were now embroiled in a vicious online battle. And when Teresa was attacked, she came back harder. She doubled down, claiming she had sources and proof of Evan cheating. Her followers came after me savagely. Shortly before the reunion was filmed in April 2021, she went on Andy Cohen's talk show and implied she had evidence of Evan cheating.

Everywhere I turned, someone was coming after me. The public was slamming me on social media, Twitter accounts were dragging Evan's name through the mud, and our children were hearing about it from their friends at school. My daughter went to bed crying at night, and Evan, who'd been satisfied enough with Teresa's half-assed apology during filming, was enraged once again and terrified about what else she'd say. But the worst beating I got was the one I took from within.

I can't control this, I can't stop this. My body was a sea of anxiety, fear, and guilt. From August 2020 to April 2021, my world was a playground on fire, and the only thing I could control was what I put inside my body. I felt better when I was starving, like it was the only way to pay for all the hurt I blamed myself for causing, so I controlled my diet like crazy. I tightened my restrictions, stopping short of the amounts I was entitled to eat, especially during freedom meals. Sometimes I skipped meals altogether just to punish myself, to take away the enjoyment of eating and leave myself hungry. I was compulsive about my record book. Every bite, every calorie, every entry into my food journal was pristine and perfect. I drew the lines of my food diary against a ruler and used only blue pen, so it was uniform and flawless. Keeping perfect control of my record book made me feel I was keeping it together, like everything wasn't falling apart. I ate as little as I could. I starved myself to feel the hunger, because the pain of starvation hurt so much it could numb the pain of everything else.

But sometimes life has a funny way of working out. During the summer of 2020, Teresa started dating a new man, Louis, and had fallen madly in love by the time we filmed our reunion in April 2021. Just before the reunion, a lot of bad press seemed to come out about him, including scathing allegations of mistreatment from his ex and information about a police report of an alleged road-rage incident involving a physical assault by Louis on the other driver (Louis has denied these allegations). I was now in a position to throw a ton of rumors *and* the accompanying news stories right back at her. Obviously wanting to avoid that, she came into the reunion like a different person, acknowledging on camera that there was no truth to the cheating rumor and offering a more sincere apology in the hope of building a friendship with me. Maybe she really wanted to turn over a new leaf, or maybe she was just protecting the man she loved from being humiliated, but either way, our public battle was over. She and Evan hugged onstage, and we agreed to put it all behind us. All that mattered to me was ending this saga in a way that made my husband happy, and now he finally was.

But the damage was done. By the time we started to discuss my next season, I was in a body that I hadn't seen in years. *I know this body, I've missed you.* It was like smelling a perfume you'd worn years before: seeing my body took me back to a different time in my life, a time when I was at my unhealthiest. And for some sick reason, even knowing how unhealthy that skeletal body was, I found it comforting, like proof that I had punished myself enough, proof that I wasn't out of control, proof that I could still be the best at something even if that was just being the thinnest person I could be. I had those pointy shoulders again and hip bones that you could see through my pants. I ran my hands down my sides and felt every rib barely concealed by my skin. I knew I was once again on a very dangerous path, and I had no idea how to get off, because I didn't want to gain anything back.

Weight consumed my thoughts more voraciously than it had in years. *Does my weight loss this year give me the freedom to eat a little more now, since I can afford to put some back?* I would have loved to do that, but I couldn't wrap my mind around gaining weight. I couldn't physically bring the food to my lips and eat it. Gaining weight was uncomfortable for me no matter how thin I was, because every pound felt like the start of an uncontrollable spiral. I didn't know how to be fine with watching the numbers climb on the scale, or how to be flexible with my size, so I did what I could to keep that weight off.

In the early spring of 2021, a few weeks after the filming the reunion, I developed a mild pain in the back of my right leg that eventually turned into a stinging throb, but I didn't know why. It wouldn't go away—not surprising when you work out hard seven days a week. It wasn't the kind of pain I couldn't push through, but it was getting worse every day, and eventually, it was too bad to ignore.

"Make sure you ice it and take a few days off from running," Evan told me. *Yeah, not happening, babe. Don't you know me by now?*

The orthopedist I saw, hoping to get a quick cortisone shot, told me the same thing. "You have tendinitis that's causing all the swelling and pain," he said. "It'll get worse if you don't take care of it. You need to rest it and ice it as much as possible." I nodded my lying head. I didn't listen, since skipping my workouts was nonnegotiable, and as the aching in my hamstring got worse, running felt like being electrocuted for thirty-minute stretches.

One May morning, a month before the new season was to start filming, I walked to my treadmill, dragging my leg behind me. I got on. I squeezed my eyes shut, opened them hard, and started to run. I bit my lower lip to mute the stinging. I let my eyes fill with tears and my chest lose its breath, and I kept running. The second I hit the thirty-minute mark, I pulled the emergency cord and buckled on the floor in agony. I had pushed through hell as hard as I could push, I had destroyed myself until my energy turned to fumes, my body wasted away, and pain shot through my eyes. When my body fell to the floor, I collapsed into a new rock bottom. I knew instantly that I couldn't do this for much longer or I'd probably kill myself trying.

I dropped my head to the ground and touched my throbbing leg and lay still for several minutes, alone on my basement floor. *How many more years can I do this?* I held on to my leg as the throb began to slow. *Will I still be doing this when I'm sixty-five? Will I even make it to sixty-five?* For the very first time, I wondered what would happen if I stopped—if I didn't run for a few days and if I started eating a little more. What if I gave myself a break from all of this? I could admit how sick I was and ask for help. *There has to be someone who can help me.*

I couldn't stop thinking *what if.* But I also knew my track record when it came to getting help. I'd promised myself before that

I would try to get better, that I'd find a doctor or a specialist who could get me out of these dangerous habits, but I had never followed through. I'd make myself promises, and then I'd make excuses and rationalize my toxic behaviors so that I could hold on to being thin as long as possible. After eighteen years of battling an eating disorder, I'd never taken any meaningful steps toward recovery. I'd never been able to let go of anorexia when I was the only one holding myself accountable.

But what if the whole world held me accountable? I knew that would change everything. If the world was watching, I wouldn't show people that there's no way out.

know what I want to focus on this season," I told Evan in the kitchen one morning a few weeks later. "I'll talk to you about it tonight."

Evan was nervous, of course. For nearly an entire season, *he* had been the storyline on a platform he'd never wanted in the first place. He was more adamant than ever about staying out of the show's drama. But beyond the PTSD of seasons past, he was also an inherently private person. He didn't want our kids' growing pains or his personal life to play out on the show.

That evening we sat down together to discuss my idea. I had thought about what I'd say, but when we were face-to-face, I didn't know where to start. Instead, I told him the truth.

"Evan, I'm really sick."

He held my gaze and nodded softly, and I could tell that he knew exactly what I meant. I could tell he'd been waiting for this day, praying that I'd get here on my own, because no one else could ever make me stop hurting myself. Evan sat completely still, waiting for me to find the rest of my words. I didn't elaborate much, because I didn't need to.

"I don't want to do this to myself anymore."

I explained that if I came clean on the show about having an eating disorder, if I told the world I needed help and let them watch me enter a recovery program on national television, I might finally follow through.

I wasn't sure how he'd react. I knew Evan wanted the best for my health, but he's never loved oversharing, especially on medical matters. Maybe this was too much, or maybe he wouldn't want our kids to see it or the whole town to discuss it in whispers behind our backs. Maybe he'd worry that the world would judge him for not saving me.

Instead, he grabbed my hands and stared at me.

"I think that sounds perfect," he said. "It's perfect. I'm so proud of you." I didn't say anything else. I didn't share all my dark secrets or confess my starvation tactics, I didn't admit that I was terrified of new foods and that eating filled me with unrelenting guilt. I didn't tell him that I worried no one would love me anymore if I gained weight. I just told him that I was finally ready to recover.

And with that, there was no turning back.

Not that I didn't *think* about turning back. In fact, for the next four weeks, I thought about it constantly. I had spent so many years being the thinnest person most people knew that it had become my identity. Jackie was the thin one. No matter what happened with family or professional success, I knew that when I walked into the room, I'd probably be the skinniest person there, and because of that, there would always be something that made me special. If I could fit into a size 00, if I were emaciated, my tiny body would keep me from ever going unnoticed. Like my high school classmate had said, everyone would always want me as long as they could pick me up with their pinkie.

Recovery felt like a death sentence for the person I had sacrificed my life to become. I'd been desperate to be thin since I was thirteen, and now here I was, ready to give it all back. *Maybe I can't do this. Maybe I'm not ready.* I went back and forth incessantly.

I thought about my clothes. All the tiny pants lining my closets and minuscule shirts folded into my drawers. *What the hell will I do with all of my clothes? What am I gonna wear?* I worried that extra fat growing on the sides of my feet would make my shoes too tight, that my fingers would get too big for my rings. I touched my spine and ran my hands down my arms. *I'll miss my bony arms. How much weight will they make me gain? What will they make me eat?* When the thought of recovery made me gag with anxiety, "they" was everyone who wanted to destroy me, who rooted against me and wanted me to be fat and not special anymore. It was them versus me. *How do I even start?* I was terrified.

Back in 2006, during the height of some of my most toxic habits and when I was three years into living in a world filled with secrets, HBO debuted a film called *Thin*. It was about a group of anorexic women, dangerously underweight, who checked themselves in to an eating disorder treatment center. I watched it like a teenage boy watching porn, terrified of being caught, mesmerized by the bodies on my screen, and studying their behaviors with nervous anticipation. *They're worse than I am, I don't do the things they do.* I told myself I wasn't like these women, but I knew I was, and I couldn't look away because the only hope I had was that they stayed alive. *They're thinner than I am, they eat less than I do, and they're still alive.* It was the only thing that made me feel like I was fine.

I don't remember a lot about the film aside from how emaciated the women were, but I'll always remember the name of the treatment center they went to. The name tucked itself into a corner of my brain, where it lived covered in thick blankets of fear, hidden away by the swaths of lies that I told myself about weight and self-worth and what makes someone beautiful, but it never left. That name stayed there waiting, the place they went to in the movie when it got so bad that the women stood on the verge of death. I never googled the place or asked questions about it because the name felt too heavy, too terrifying. I didn't know anything else about it, but I knew it was called Renfrew.

"I've relapsed with my eating disorder," I told the producers a few days later over Zoom. I had never recovered from anorexia in the first place, so I couldn't really relapse; but I had gotten better at hiding it, and I weighed more than I had at the height of my sickness, so instead of explaining how I'd functioned for the last ten years, I found it easier to explain my increasingly restrictive habits and decreasing weight as a relapse. "I want to stop. I want to go to therapy and recover on the show."

They loved it, not just as a focus for me on the show, but to help save my life. When they asked if I knew where to call, I told them I did. "There's a place called Renfrew," I said.

Before any of the actual stuff of recovery could happen, I'd have to explain the situation on camera. I was scared that telling my castmates or my parents would lead to questions I couldn't answer or pressure to heal faster than I was capable of healing.

In the movies and on TV, when someone goes into recovery, things often follow a seamless beaten path. The protagonist struggles, hits rock bottom, goes into rehab, and then BOOM—they're healed. The epiphanies and aha moments all happen fast, in healing group discussions amid a circle of chairs, and before you know it, the character is navigating life in a healthy new world. That's often not the way it happens in real life. I realized that right away, from the day I decided to get help, when the crushing fears and relentless self-doubt set in over whether I was even capable of recovery. People don't want to see baby steps and regressions when the entertainment world has always fed them speedy redemption stories. As much as I wanted this illness behind me, the thought of eating and gaining weight was horrifying, and I knew the process—my process—would be slow. I needed it to go slow. It was the one thing that televising my recovery made me worry about: the world would expect me to recover quickly.

I knew that once I unlocked the gate holding all my secrets, a lifetime of confessions about toxic behaviors and crushing self-doubt might spill out. I wanted only Evan standing in the monsoon with me. I'd tell him about my recovery plans over drinks, and I'd let it be filmed for the show.

Drinks were my favorite type of plans, because I never felt too much pressure to eat at happy hour—turning down food before dinner was pretty easy to normalize. But drinks had to be early enough that they didn't linger into dinnertime, when people would start ordering appetizers and expecting me to share. When I asked

Evan to go for drinks so we could film a date scene, I made sure we went at five p.m. The scene was mostly about what we'd do with our free time while our kids were away at a two-week sports camp, but I'd also be telling Evan that I finally wanted to get professional help for my eating disorder. I had already told him I wanted to get help, but when I'd sat with him weeks earlier, I hadn't let him in on any secrets or told him how anorexia had seeped into every part of my life. He didn't know anything yet.

Evan never asked questions about my eating disorder or my weight, even when I was at my worst, in the mid-2000s or now, as my body turned frail once again. It would be easy to say that he could have tried harder, that as my husband, he should have shaken me and cried, he should have told me he needed to help me, that he'd do anything to help me. But how could I expect someone else to save me when I refused to save myself? When Evan brought up food, I shut him down instantly; when he offered me food, I got mad and said no. When he mentioned weight, I aggressively walked out of the room. If he'd grabbed me and shaken me, I would have pulled away, and we both knew that. I was an adult, a stubborn adult who lied to him and everyone else about my health, and if doctors thought I was fine, I can't blame Evan for believing I was at least physically okay. My eating disorder was not up for discussion, so I didn't expect him to discuss it. Evan had said enough over the years that I knew if I ever found the strength to get here, he'd be waiting, ready to help me. I always knew he'd do anything to help me, even if he never pleaded with me to get better.

Besides, I was so embarrassed of the things I had done. My

confessions were buried in shame, unable to reach the surface and find voice. I never wanted Evan to know the details of my sickness or the depths of my fears. I worried he'd think I was crazy, that this woman he thought was intelligent and sane, the woman raising his children and sleeping next to him at night, was actually overflowing with ridiculous thoughts. Until right now, all the secrets were still mine.

At least that's what I told myself. If I could believe that Evan was in the dark about my obsessive dieting, food anxiety, and toxic habits, I could keep going. If there were no victims of my anorexia aside from me, I could justify its purpose in my life. It gave me peace, made me pretty, kept me "in shape," and it was mine. I unwittingly flaunted my eating disorder right in his face with the measuring spoons and journals and size-o clothing. I paraded it with my fiber bars and fake breads and the glass bathroom scale that I treated like a delicate Fabergé egg. I flaunted my anorexia and told myself that he had no idea what I was doing. I had to tell myself that story. I couldn't face the reality that my husband was watching me destroy myself, knowing that I'd explode if he said anything about any of it. I didn't want Evan to save me, and I made that crystal-clear. It was a lose-lose position for him.

He ordered food during our filmed happy hour, which I quickly declined to share. "It's five o'clock," I said, trying my best to make it seem like ordering food at five was so ridiculous as to be gluttonous. "You go for it." If I could take any food responsibilities off myself, and let people know that my *lack of hunger* shouldn't hold them back from eating whatever they wanted, I felt no guilt about my behavior. It wasn't hurting anyone else.

We started talking about our life before kids, when we ran around the city like free spirits, and I asked Evan if he remembered the time we went to a bar to meet his friend.

"When you fainted?" he asked without missing a beat.

There had been hundreds of nights when we'd gone to bars to meet up with friends, but that night had clearly left a scar, one that we'd never dared talk about until now. I told Evan I hadn't eaten that day, and when he asked me why, I opened up—just a crack—giving the most rudimentary of explanations of how anorexia took over my life. "I got from a place where I didn't eat anything . . . to a place where I could eat what I wanted two or three times a week, and I thought I was cured," I told him.

I knew I was lying—I had never thought I was cured. I wanted to be done lying, but where do you start when the truth is buried under so much shame and fear? "I don't know," I said. "I'm not okay." Evan sat quietly, his eyes focused on mine, as he waited for me to figure out what to reveal.

I explained that losing weight over the past year had made me happy even though I was underweight, and I was tired of all the rituals that went into eating. God, there was so much more to say, but my mind was exhausted. I thought he would nod in under-standing, offer me support, and end the scene by telling me he loved me, like he had on the couch a few weeks back. But that's not what happened.

"Our kids notice it, by the way," he said.

Wait . . . WHAT? *I've been hiding everything so carefully. How can my kids notice anything when the adults in my life don't even notice?* I was trying desperately to control the conversation, the way I tried to control everything that had to do with food or weight, but Evan took the wheel.

"They said, 'Why is Mom eating the same dinner every night?' and I said, 'Just let her be.'"

Evan had just told the world that I had normalized distorted eating for my children. And then he told the world that I had made it so hard to help me that even he'd had no choice but to let it happen. I wanted so badly for this to be a heroic story, but it wasn't. It was the story about a woman who was continuing a horrible cycle of disordered eating for the next generation of her family. I felt like a monster.

I stared at his food and noticed all the veins on my bony hands. I was famished. I wanted to stop everything right there, smash my fork into his seafood salad, say a final fuck-you to the emptiness in my stomach, and just eat, but I was nowhere near that mental place. My eyes welled as I realized how my addiction to dieting and thinness had spilled over to the people I loved, especially the ones I had been put on earth to guide through life.

"I'm sorry," I said through tears as I thought about everyone I'd hurt, all the ones I'd forced to watch me hurt myself as I made them stand idly by. "I know it's weird to have a wife who doesn't eat."

Evan was sorry, too.

"I didn't know how to help you—"

He told me he'd be with me every step of the way.

"I'm your partner," he said. "If you hurt, I hurt."

And with that, my journey into recovery began.

If I was going to do it publicly, I couldn't keep any more secrets. There would be no more hiding or shame. I thought about myself at thirty years old, wearing child-size clothing, shivering with blue lips, and eating oatmeal off the side of a straw, watching a movie about anorexics—the one where the women went to Renfrew—looking for answers to questions that I had no one to ask. *How does this end? How do I get out of this before I die?* And here I was, fifteen years later, with an opportunity to tell my story and reach millions of people with eating disorders who feel so incredibly alone and assume they're the only ones suffering the way they do. A chance to reach people who are so lost in distorted eating that they feel like there's no hope for recovery. If that sounds self-righteous or self-important, I don't fucking care. I knew what I needed back then, and it was exactly what I wanted to give to anyone who needed it now. A recovery story. Hope. The tiniest of road maps for their journey out and back into the world. Maybe other people knew better ways to help, more effective ways to get people to recover from this god-awful illness. Maybe other people could offer treatment plans and therapy and counseling groups, but this was all I knew how to do. All I could do was offer hope, but I could do it on a worldwide stage.

A few weeks later, I arrived with a camera crew in tow at the Renfrew Center of Northern New Jersey.

CHAPTER NINE

❧

TAKE ME TO THE OTHER SIDE

You don't drown by falling in water. You drown by staying there.

—Anonymous

I stood in the hallway outside the Renfrew Center's entrance, staring at the name on the door. It was a place I'd always thought of as a final resort, a purgatory for the sickest of the sick. A place you go when death is your next step, but you've caught yourself—or someone else caught you—just in time. Renfrew didn't seem that scary as I stood in front of it in the daylight. Nonetheless, I was afraid, and a million worries flooded my head. I wondered if this was my last day of being thin.

I wanted this so badly—I wanted to be normal and finally live and eat like a normal person, whatever that meant. I wanted my children to have a normal mother and Evan to have a normal wife. I needed to stop torturing myself, but I was terrified of what eating might do to me and how quickly it would make me fat again. I ran my fingers over my shoulder blades as I waited to go inside and film my intake meeting for the show. Feeling my bones always calmed me down. Feeling them spike through my skin always let me know that nothing had happened yet. I hadn't spiraled, I was still thin, still safe.

Half of me wanted to burst through the doors, confess every toxic secret I'd been keeping for two decades, and stay there until I was cured, but the other half of me felt like I was entering a tunnel with no idea where it would lead or if I'd make it through. As grueling as anorexia was, as much as I dreaded the physical pain and the mind-crippling anxiety, my eating disorder was also my safety net. It kept me from being the person I had been before, when nobody seemed to care if I was there or not, when nobody thought I was special, especially me. When I was heavier, I thought nobody saw who I was, only who I could be *if she could just some lose weight*. I wrapped myself inside an eating disorder and I lived there, in its grips. I let it control me, and in return, it gave me what I'd always wanted—to be thin, to be noticed and valued in a world that celebrates being skinny. Anorexia let me believe I was a new person, so I starved myself, surrendering my body and soul to the world of diet culture in order to be somebody else. I gave up eating, and in return the world told me I was beautiful.

As I stood outside of Renfrew's doors, everything was still black and white. There was thin or fat; happy or sad; beautiful or invisible. *What's the weight of in-between?* I didn't know what would happen next, but I knew I couldn't live with anorexia any longer, because the price I was paying was too high. I had lost so many years to starvation. I had lost so many celebrations with loved ones, so many dinners where I thought about nothing but calories, where conversations became background noise as my eyes glazed over and my mind did math. I had lost so many moments with my children because I was too hungry to think of anything but going home to find something safe to eat. I'd lost anniversaries and birthdays, I'd lost Valentine's Days, Thanksgivings, and countless vacations, and I could never redo any of them. But I wouldn't give anorexia any more of my life, not another day in any of the years I had left. I was terrified, though at the same time, I'd never felt more ready to let go of it all.

The intake coordinator was a young woman named Christen who led me into a small room with a desk and a couch. As I walked behind her, I suddenly worried that I didn't look thin enough to be there. *I'm wasting their time,* I thought as I stared at my arms, as thin and veiny as they were, and worried they looked too ordinary for someone who claimed to be sick. *I'm wearing 24-inch waist jeans, that's not so small,* I thought. *Maybe I don't belong here.* I knew that dieting consumed my world and that I was eating the smallest amount I could survive on, but I also knew that ever since I'd had children, I hadn't looked *danger-zone* thin. I had to starve to maintain my current body, and getting thinner than that would require me to cut out even more food, which I wouldn't know how to do.

What does anorexia look like? I didn't look the way people might expect someone with the disorder to look. Media tells us that we're emaciated, skin and bones, sickly and weak. Our hair is thin, and our faces are pale and drawn. TV shows and movies tell people there's no question whether an anorexic person is sick, you can look at us and tell, you can break us in half. Anorexics on TV don't look like me—thin but not *scary thin*—eating the occasional meal, like meat and potatoes. *Anorexic people don't eat meat and potatoes.* I knew the world thought like that, and that's how I was able to keep going for so long. I no longer looked like I had at my wedding, frail and deathly, and I didn't wear children's clothing anymore—but my habits were just the same, even with those two chaotic "freedom meals" a week, and my disorder was just as strong as it was then.

As I sat down on the couch, I felt the sharp discomfort of air-conditioning blowing from the ceiling, and I thought about the fiber snacks in my bag and wondered how long until I could secretly devour them in my car.

"The first thing we'll talk about is your medical history and your eating patterns, in detail," Christen said. My mind flashed to my children, the way they'd been noticing my habits. *No more secrets,* I whispered in my head. *No more lies.* The things I was about to tell Christen were so disordered, I wondered if some of them might be things she'd never heard before. I wasn't worried about exposing my secrets to the world, I just worried about saving myself. *I have to tell her everything,* I thought. This was my best chance to break free from anorexia, before I let it go any further in the direction it was going. I needed to dive in so deeply and confess so intensely that if I didn't have the strength to save myself and my fears left me drowning in sickness, someone would know to come save me.

I told Christen everything. I told her about all of my rules, the shatterproof guidelines that dictated when I was *entitled* to eat, and all of the empty garbage I used to shut off hunger. I told her about the games I played with food, breaking up my freedom meals so people could see me eat, freezing things that no one would think to freeze so I could scrape them instead of chewing, and the sick foods

I ate when no one was watching. I explained that when I did eat something, the only requirements were that it be edible and low-calorie, even if it was filled with chemicals and artificial sweeteners, because I was eating with the sole purpose of filling myself enough so I could go about life without falling over.

I explained to Christen all the ways that my diet was devoid of nutrition. I told her about all the Jell-O, and the mountains of fiber, and the massive Tupperware containers filled with lettuce and salt that I consumed to fill me up. If something resembled food enough for me to eat and keep my organs functioning while I remained thin, I could eat it. I also told her about how I pushed myself seven days a week to exercise, sweating until I couldn't see straight, with virtually no days off, even when I was sick.

What was captured on the show was shocking enough for a world in which most people don't understand how eating disorders work. Unless you're one of the thirty million Americans who has an eating disorder, my answers probably sounded harrowing and unrelatable and left no question about why I was there. It was clear that I was deeply anorexic and needed help. I spoke calmly, but I felt desperate to start something, anything, that could help me to begin crawling out.

Christen measured my heart rate three times to make sure her number was right. "That's really low," she said after the first mea-surement and the second, but I told her it had been that way for-ever. "It's because I run," I said, repeating the words of every doctor who'd ever measured my sluggish heart. I couldn't understand why she seemed so worried about that; the numbers were no different from what they usually were: 43, 41, 43. "Okay," she told me as she made notes at her desk. She looked up. "A slow heart rate is often a symptom of malnourishment," she said.

But that's not why MY heart rate is slow, I thought. *I never hurt my heart from dieting. I wouldn't do that to my children.*

Denial had been driving this illness from the very start. I'd spent years denying hunger, denying signs that my body needed nutrients, denying the reality of what my children were learning from my behavior. Now I was denying what a medical expert was telling me about my heart. I couldn't accept the truth because it was too painful to think that I could have already done such significant damage to myself. I wanted to scream it out loud, as cameras watched my reaction, so the world wouldn't think I was a selfish woman who could have destroyed my family and killed myself to be thin. But I sat quietly as my desperation turned to anger and I realized how many health professionals allowed me to walk out of their offices underweight, with a heart that was struggling to beat.

Christen explained that because my diet had no nutrients, increasing my food intake would increase my circulation, which could overwhelm my heart and other organs. I had never heard anything like that before. "Some people experience heart attacks or cardiac issues," she said as I froze in silence.

I suddenly understood why people die from eating disorders. I later learned that someone dies from a complication of an eating disorder every 52 minutes, over 10,000 deaths in the U.S. each year alone, with anorexia having the highest mortality rate of all eating disorders. One third of deaths in anorexic patients are from cardiac issues like a slow heart rate (bradycardia) and low blood pressure (hypotension).* I had both, and my doctors never worried, never asked questions, never tried to help me. My doctors were never concerned about me being too thin, only about me being too fat.

It took eighteen years of compliments about my tiny figure, eighteen years of rationalizations and excuses, countless doctors ignoring all the signs of anorexia, and friends and family I'd admonished into silence, all those years for me to realize that I could have really died from this—not in theory, and not at some distant point in the future, but on any given day since 2003. *How could I let this go so far? Why would I do this to myself?* I thought about the way I ran for miles every day, pushing my body past its limits, heaving for air, and sending my heart rate soaring. I wondered how close I'd come to a having a heart attack. There were days when I'd had chest pains and workouts when I'd struggled terribly to breathe. *Did I get that close?* I was angry and ashamed, but most of all, I was afraid.

"We think residential treatment is the best option at this point," said the Renfrew clinician who called me not long after my intake appointment, after seeing the results of my physical. "We think you'd benefit the most from an intensive inpatient program." Even though I knew she was right, I also knew I couldn't do that. I think this was hard for some viewers to understand, and it was hard for me to explain, but I didn't want my recovery to feel rushed or like a punishment. I didn't want to feel desperate to get it over with so I could go back to my children and my life. I needed recovery to be a part of my everyday life. I wanted to set an example for anyone watching, but I also needed to make decisions that I could

---

* https://www.verywellmind.com/yes-eating-disorders-can-be-deadly-1138269

follow through on. Evan had told me to go—he'd handle the house and the kids—but I couldn't bring myself to do it. I was open to intense therapy, as much as I needed, but I couldn't agree to live in a treatment center when my four young children needed me at home. Inpatient treatment meant leaving New Jersey for at least a few months, since the local Renfrew Center was outpatient only, and I felt like leaving my family would destroy me.

I knew there were other options, and I swore to myself at that moment to do anything and everything I could do to get better as long as I could stay with my family. "Please help me find a therapist," I begged the clinician over the phone. "I swear I'm committed to this, I promise I'll go to therapy as much as you tell me to, I just need to be home."

Christen sent me the names of a few outpatient therapists Renfrew worked with, and I had a call with Ilene, my new eating disorder psychotherapist, the next day. When I sat down in Ilene's office to begin therapy, I didn't even notice the cameras or microphones that I allowed into the room. Nothing I did from that point on was for any purpose other than recovering.

In the very first moments of therapy, as had happened at Renfrew, I felt an urge to hold on, like I was standing in the center of a field on a winter day, wrapped in a thousand blankets of disordered eating habits, and one by one, they were being pulled off of my body as I spun in a circle until I was left naked, freezing, with nothing to keep me warm or safe. *Let me keep a few bad habits,* I thought. *I can get rid of almost everything, but I just need to keep a few.*

"I can't make you do anything," Ilene told me from the start, sensing the anxiety in my voice. "Tell me what you're afraid of."

Where do I even begin? I thought. "I'm afraid of losing control," I said as the tears began falling. "It takes so much work. I see what my calendar has on it, and I worry which days will require me to eat and which days will require me to fake it. It's all day, every day." I could tell by her calm reaction that she'd heard it all before, and for the first time, I felt a little less alone. I felt like it wasn't *only me* who lived in this sickening world, and it wasn't only me who had to fight to make it out alive. "My body hurts, and I do it anyway."

Ilene understood my fears and knew what to say. "You're not supposed to have to suffer like this," she told me. I knew she was right, *but how do you stop a runaway train?* When she asked if Evan had tried to help me, I told her how I'd pushed him away. "I said no, please leave me alone, I'm fine, but I was all alone with all of this in my head, and I didn't know anyone could help me," I told her. I was so terrified of food and what it might do to me, I wouldn't even let myself think about getting help, much less letting other people help me.

"Do you think your kids know that you're suffering?" she asked. Yes, I told her, I know they do. "I always thought I was being very sleuth, except when I took them out to eat," I said. "I've never gotten ice cream with them, not in the hundreds of times I've taken them for ice cream." Voices started screaming inside my head. *Now you're gonna have to eat ice cream in front of the world. Slow the hell down.*

"When was the last time you had ice cream?" Ilene asked. I guessed twenty years, but it had definitely been longer. It was before my Tasti D-Lite diet in the late nineties, before I moved to New York and tried everything to become one of those women I envied whose pants gaped at the waist when they tucked in their shirts. The last time I'd had actual ice cream was in the early nineties. The last time I had eaten it without guilt, I was a child. "Would that be a good goal this week?" she asked. *Don't say yes, don't commit, don't say you'll do it.*

I wanted to say yes, but I didn't know how to eat ice cream. Sounds strange, but I just couldn't imagine actually *doing it.* I didn't know how to get to the point where ice cream could go in my mouth and be swallowed into my stomach instead of spat back into a napkin. "I don't even know how to do that," I cried. "It's so stupid." In that moment, I felt stupid. *Stupid stupid stupid.* I worried that no one would understand. "I get that you're really scared," Ilene said gently, "but this would be really powerful in terms of helping your kids." She reminded me why I was there, to finally free myself, to give my children a healthy mother, and to take back my life. "You need to start eating more, and this is how we start to expand your world," she said. "Remember, you're not compensating for the ice cream," she added. "This is not instead of, this is extra."

I was so nervous about eating ice cream that I played the scene over in my head a million times before it happened. I wondered if my children would notice or if they'd even care. *Maybe they don't give a shit whether I eat with them or not, maybe I'm overreacting about all of this, maybe I'm not so sick, and I'm just making a big deal over nothing.* But when I thought about actually eating, I snapped back to reality. Anorexia still controlled everything. *I want my babies to care,* I thought. *I need this to be worth it.*

The next day, late on a summer afternoon, I piled my kids into the car and told them we were going for ice cream, as I'd done a million times before. I also told them we'd be filming it for the show, but they didn't seem to care about that. When we got to the ice cream parlor, I let my children place their orders as usual. Then I asked them a question they'd never heard before. "Should Mommy get ice cream?" I watched their faces: I wanted them to cheer, I wanted bursts of excitement, arms wrapped around my waist in joy and looks of astonishment, but I only got "Yes."

If no one really cares, why am I doing this? Why am I eating something as awful as ice cream when I don't even want it? "Get strawberry," one of my kids piped up. "Get vanilla," said another. I watched in horror as the server piled the small cup three inches over the top. *Stop, stop, it's enough,* I wanted to shout. It was too much food, but I took the cup and walked outside.

We sat down at an outdoor table, and my children started to eat. I looked at my ice cream. *This is it,* I thought. In eighteen years, this was the first bite I'd take of anything that deviated from the rules of how I was allowed to eat. I hesitated, but then I realized a simple truth: *The only way to start eating . . . is to eat.*

"I don't think Mom likes it," Hudson said in the moments after I took my first bite. I could hear the hope in his voice, as subtle as it was. *My children need me to like it.* They needed me to enjoy sharing in these moments with them. And all my demons aside, it tasted like heaven. "It's so good," I said, nearly moaning as their eyes lit up, watching me. I don't think they understood what was happening—why I had suddenly decided to start eating ice cream and, if I liked it this much, why I hadn't eaten it all along. I'd need to explain it to them, one day. I knew that I'd already done so much damage to my kids; I'd sent them so many awful messages about food and dieting, extreme thinness, and brutal exercise. One day I'd need to start trying to undo it all, if that was even possible.

But on this day, I would just relish the experience with my children. When they lifted their spoon and offered me a bite, I said, "Thank you, baby, I'd love a bite." We laughed and shared; they watched me eating ice cream. My kids didn't cheer or wrap their arms around me in amazement, but they didn't have to. What I saw on their faces was connection, it was love, it was relief. It was everything I needed it to be.

I wish I could tell you that the feelings lasted. I finished half of my small cup, and almost immediately after my last bite, the guilt crept in, and by the time I got home, I was consumed with worry about how my body would react. I had underestimated how hard it would be not to compensate for eating something "bad." *Am I supposed to pretend that the ice cream situation didn't just happen?* I kept closing my eyes to think about how much of the oversize serving I had consumed, how many calories could be in a cup that size, how I'd destroyed my carefully calculated diet. My compulsion to count and calculate and undo the damage was crushing, and every bit of food I looked at for the rest of the day felt unnecessary and gluttonous.

But I *didn't* do a damn thing about it, and that's how I knew this time was different. I pushed the voices aside and ate my disordered dinner as usual; I didn't allow myself to Google the calories in ice cream and write them in a book. Instead, I chose this one tiny step toward recovery. That's all I could ask of myself. I just needed to start to get better, and I had started.

Here's something most people don't know about reality television: the best storylines often come full circle. There's a beginning, a middle, and an end, and when the season is over, the ideal storyline ties a bow (even a loosely tied bow) on a situation, letting the viewers feel some closure so we can all move forward to other things. Looking back at Season 11 of *RHONJ,* I think that's what the ice cream scene represented to a lot of people who either struggled with an eating disorder or loved someone who was struggling. When the season started, I was anorexic; in the middle, I got treatment; and in the end, lo and behold, I ate ice cream. *Ta-da.* It was quick, it was happy, and it gave people hope. Maybe their loved ones, or they themselves, could find the strength to eat ice cream, too.

But when the cameras went down, my recovery journey was only beginning.

I wanted to understand how I had gotten so sick, and why I stayed this way for so long. *What went so wrong in my life that starving myself became the answer?* "Society teaches us that thinner is better and that it's something people respect and admire," Ilene explained. "After all the pain and rejection and the bullying, you wanted that more than anything. You wanted to feel worthy and valuable and desirable, and society tells us this is the way to do it." I knew she was right, but it didn't make me want to get better. If anything, I was even more scared to let go of what society thought was perfect, the rail-thin body everyone noticed. *If this disorder has given me what I was always chasing, why would I give it all back?* "Anorexia is self-protection by way of self-destruction," she told me. "But it feels like the perfect fix, and that's why it's so hard to let go of."

Ilene suggested we start combating my fear of food by adding "extras" to my diet each day and not compensating for them. As scary as that was, the joy of eating something extra every day was intoxicating. But then the anorexia would take over. I'd dream about what "extra" thing I'd eat, how big it should be, what time I should eat it, who I should eat it with, who should see me eating it so they'd know I was getting better, whether I should save the extra for the next day so I could have two extras or a double portion of extras instead of one. And if I got to the end of the day without eating an extra, I couldn't decide whether I had won or failed. That was not the way it was supposed to work. I couldn't make sense of the extras. *Why is this so frustrating? Is eating supposed to be this hard?*

The first full month of recovery wasn't great. Every bite I took set off waves of guilt. When I tried to eat, the voices inside my head screamed to slow down. *You don't need to go so fast, you don't need to eat that.* Sometimes I'd stare at food in the grocery store, wondering if it was too much, picking it up and putting it down over and over. One day I bought a tuna sandwich for lunch, determined to eat half, but when I opened it, I instinctively tossed a huge chunk of tuna into a napkin, squeezed it flat in my palm, and threw it away. *I wouldn't notice that chunk anyway,* I reasoned, *and I saved an easy 50 calories.* I cut food into quarters when eating half made my head spin, and I threw things away before I was finished to prove I still had self-control. I'd buy new foods to take home and I'd dissect them, pulling out parts that might send me over the edge, scraping mayonnaise off bread and picking excess avocado slices out of salads. *There's nothing wrong with being thin,* the voices insisted. *People just want you to fail.*

At the start of the second month, Ilene recommended a specialized medical dietician for me to work with. I committed to two sessions of therapy and a session of nutrition counseling every week, with no exceptions. My dietician took over the role of food counseling, and my therapist got to the business of uncovering the root of my anorexia and why I was holding on to it.

Twice a week, Ilene and I talked about all the things I'd never talked about that stayed inside my head and ate away at my soul. We talked about all the years I'd spent running away from myself, from the sixteen-year-old girl who nobody cared was in the room, who nobody thought was beautiful.

We talked about my terrible habits, the ways I tortured myself, the ways I forced myself to suffer. I was honest and unfiltered with her, and she never flinched. Ilene called the voices my "internal tyrant" that drove my actions and controlled my world. The internal tyrant made me feel like I needed to prove myself to people through success, through the way I looked, through the number on a scale. I needed to prove everyone wrong about the person they thought I was. "You took all of your drive and your energy, and you put it all toward this goal of being thin, and you got really good at anorexia," she said. "That tyrant tells you you're not good enough, that you'll never be good enough, and so you become incredibly self-critical for fear that someone will find something they can criticize about you."

When you live in a smaller body, she explained, it feels like there's less to criticize. "Silencing that internal tyrant is key for recovery."

As the months went on, we talked about self-esteem, high school, self-compassion, confidence, forgiveness, and what it means to have true quality of life. We talked and we talked, and every week, the darkness of my secret world inside anorexia slowly brightened, shards of light filtering in through growing cracks in dirty windows. My secrets were dying in the light. Every week, I understood a little more about why I had taken this path, why I accepted all the pain, why I never thought I deserved better. "If we had grown up in an ideal world where everything had gone right, we'd love ourselves and have a loving relationship with ourselves," Ilene said, "and that's what we're doing here. I'm helping you have a healthier relationship with yourself." That sense of self, of loving ourselves and knowing who we are and what our value is, that's the key to everything. "When you love and respect yourself, you won't starve yourself," she said, "because it'll be unacceptable to you to treat yourself like that."

My nutritionist, Theresa, understood my eating habits in a way that I'd never imagined someone would, often telling me how common my patterns were. That always made me feel less alone. She moved slowly, she grasped my fear without judgment, and she answered every irrational question I could ask. *Will I gain too much weight if I eat a turkey burger, will fish skin make me too heavy, is 2 percent yogurt too gluttonous?* We talked about the imperfect science of calories, the way the human body works, the counterproductive nature of diets, and the realities of metabolism. After the first week with her, I threw away my measuring spoons. "What happened to all the measuring spoons?" Jonas asked me one day after school when he needed to measure a tablespoon of baking powder for science class. "I don't measure things anymore, so I got rid of them," I said. Jonas riffled through the drawer as he mumbled annoyedly about his homework, but I didn't feel bad; I just felt proud. It was so small, but I was so damn proud.

Theresa and I talked about hunger, a feeling I didn't know what to do with. I had learned to shut off hunger like a nuisance that needed to be ignored until it went away. I didn't eat when I was hungry, I ate when I was scheduled to eat; and I didn't eat the foods I craved, I ate what I was allowed to eat. I had convinced myself that hunger was weakness, so I could rationalize ignoring it, but I was always hungry. "If I eat every time I'm hungry, I'll never stop eating," I told her. "Of course you will," she assured me. "If you eat what your body needs, you usually won't feel like eating more." Once I understood that food was no longer scarce, that I could eat anything whenever I wanted it, food stopped feeling like a forbidden pleasure, and I stopped thinking about it all the time.

Recovery moved slowly, but as the months went on, I gave myself the grace of time. I no longer felt the need to prove how fast and strong I was by recovering quicker than anyone else. Some days were good, others were bad. Some days I took two steps forward, and sometimes I stood frozen in fear, too exhausted to keep moving, for weeks at a time, until I could take my next step. But I never moved backward, not even at the worst times. I never starved myself or misused food and hunger another day in my life.

I almost never spoke to Evan about recovery during the early months. He wanted to help me, and I didn't know how to let him do that. I wasn't ready to eat his home-cooked meals or indulge in a night of Southern barbecue with him. I didn't want to replace my drenching cardio workouts by going on a hike or doing yoga together, and I was scared to disappoint him by constantly turning down his offers. Despite that, he lifted me up, unsolicited, at every turn. "I see how great you're doing, I see all the progress," he'd say on days when I felt like I'd done nothing at all. "I'm so proud of you. I'm here whenever you want to talk about it." Any time I got dressed, he'd tell me how beautiful I looked, calling me the "hottest wife in the world," and he'd always remind me that our children were watching—and noticing—that I was eating.

One day in the spring of 2022, a few months after I'd started therapy, I stood in my closet, filled with all the clothes I used to wear, and took a pair of jeans off a hanger. They were a pair I used to love, that once fit easily and beautifully, in a size I'd always coveted being. I decided to try them on to see if they'd still fit and to show myself that maybe my body hadn't changed too much. I spoke to my dietician about it all the time—about how much weight I might gain and when it might stop and where I might plateau—and even though I knew it would inevitably happen, I hadn't come to terms with my body *actually* getting that much bigger. No matter how many conversations I had with Theresa and Ilene about self-compassion and doing away with my need for external validation, about not judging myself by the size of my clothes or the number on a scale, I couldn't wrap my head around my clothes never fitting me again.

I held the jeans out in front of me, placed my right foot inside, and ran the denim up my leg until I felt it squeezing my thigh so tight that the material would no longer move. I sat down and put my left foot into the left side, standing up to pull the waistband as high as it'd go before my body stopped it from going any farther. With the waistband about three inches lower than it needed to be, I took a deep breath and sucked in as much as I could. Then I squatted down to stretch the fabric enough to make it fit. I wanted to feel like my old self for even a moment, like I was still thin and could still button my old pants.

The second I squatted down, the entire seam of the jeans tore, from the knees up the thighs and through the crotch, my body bursting through the material like it was screaming for me to stop. *This isn't you anymore, Jackie. This isn't you. You don't need to be that person anymore.* I stayed there on the floor, looking at the massive hole I'd created in the jeans I once loved, before I peeled them off and threw them in the garbage. I was finally eating, finally following through on all the promises I'd made myself, and the wreckage of denim stuffed into my trash can was the proof. I was succeeding, and yet, there on my bedroom floor, I felt like a failure.

Ilene suggested that I find an internist who specialized in eating disorders, one who knew the signs of anorexia and could treat any damage that malnourishment might have caused over the years, damage that might be overlooked by other doctors. I found just a few specialized doctors in New Jersey and only one taking new patients, with a six-month wait to be seen. So I switched to a doctor whose bio listed eating disorders and women's wellness under a long list of specialties. When I made my appointment, the receptionist asked why I wanted to see her. "I need a physical," I said, "but I'm also in recovery from an eating disorder, and I want to see someone who understands them."

When I got to the office, a nurse brought me down a hallway into a room where I sat down on the papered table as she stared at my chart, perplexed. Then she looked up with a crinkled eyebrow. "You're here because you have an eating disorder?" she asked, as if she'd never seen those words in her life. I was suddenly uncomfortable and ashamed, like I was making a big deal out of something that she clearly didn't think was a big deal. "No," I said quickly, "I'm just here for a physical." The nurse smiled and closed my chart. "Oh, okay," she said with a laugh. "I was so confused. Because you don't look like you have an eating disorder."

When she closed the door, I sat in stunned silence. *Why does this hurt so badly? I'm fat again—she said that because I'm fat again.* I let myself feel all of it, the shame, the worry about moving too fast, the fear about where my path toward recovery was headed and what I'd look like when it was over, and I began to cry. I cried because an entire identity, one I'd spent years crafting and decades maintaining in painstaking detail, was gone in a matter of months. I was no longer the thinnest person in the room, not even close, and I'd never be her again. I wasn't skinny anymore. I was no longer a question mark, and no one wondered if I'd ever modeled or whether I'd given birth to my own children—questions that used to fill me with validation and made me feel extraordinary to everyone else's average. I no longer had a body that made me stand out from the crowd, one that was never ignored. No one asked how I stayed so thin anymore. The old me was gone. I felt nothing in that moment but despair. I wasn't proud, and I didn't feel strong, I just felt like going home.

I gave myself that moment to sit in the pain. Perched on the cold plastic bed of the empty room, I cried about all the comments that I knew would continue to come, all the people who might think I gave up, about not feeling special anymore. And then the moment passed, and I thought of Ilene's voice. "We're meant to have appetites, Jackie," she'd said. "We're meant to nourish ourselves, and we're meant to eat. That's part of being a healthy human. That's part of self-love."

I made my choice when I started therapy. I chose my health and happiness, I chose my children and husband, I chose to fully enjoy my life, and I chose to love myself enough to feed my body. I chose to live without anorexia. The road would be bumpy, life would surely knock me down a few times, but I knew I'd get there eventually.

I knew that one day I'd be able to tell people how much better life is on the other side.

CHAPTER TEN

∽

CHOOSING MY ADVENTURE

Sleep offered me little solace from sickness. I'd often dream about food.

I had the same dream constantly during my eighteen years of anorexia, with the same ending and the same feelings of terror, but with different foods all the time. It went like this: I'd be drinking a giant bottle of diet soda, and as I lifted my chin to the sky, turning the bottle upside down to let the last drops hit my tongue, I'd catch sight of the label and suddenly realize that I'd drunk two liters of regular soda by mistake. I'd wake up breathless, in a state of panic. Sometimes I'd dream that I ate a veggie burger, and as I was holding my last bite, I'd glance down at the empty packaging and realize that it was beef and I had mistakenly eaten the bun. Sometimes I'd dream I'd mindlessly eaten a bag of Doritos while immersed in conversation before realizing what I had done. Every time I had this dream, the anxiety would be playing out in my body as I woke up with my heart pounding. Food terrorized me. I was so scared of gaining weight that eating became an actual nightmare.

I haven't had a dream like that since 2021. The nightmare I have now happens when I'm awake, when I think of the moment when I lay on a gym floor that same year, holding my leg and staring at the beads of sweat covering the base of the treadmill, watching them turn into streaks as they slid off the base to the floor. I lay on my back, completely malnourished and heaving in pain, and knew I was in a downward spiral again.

For years, I had my routine down to a science: how much I could eat, how I could fool people, which excuses to make in order to keep my weight the same. I stayed just underweight enough to feel special but close-to-normal enough to skirt by. Anorexia made all the rules, remaining quietly in charge, existing so discreetly that everyone else could overlook it, especially if they didn't want to see it. I became so skilled at hiding an eating disorder that I thought I could keep it secretly with me forever.

But it had started getting worse. In the months leading up to that moment, triggered by stress, I built in more rules and less food, more charts and more numbers, and stricter exercise habits. My weight started dropping, my body was hurting, and with every passing day, I was getting sicker. Anorexia constantly told me I was nothing without it, reminding me that before it found me, I was undesirable, uninvited, unnoticed. *I made you who you are,* it said. *I took you away from a life you hated.* I thought I had no choice. I thought I had to keep it forever.

As a kid in the eighties, long before dieting took over my life, I devoured a series of books in which you could choose your own adventure. Throughout the book, every so often, you could decide what your character's next step should be, which directed you to a new set of pages, changing the course of the book and leading you to a different ending with every decision. I think about that moment I was lying on the floor. What if I'd chosen a different move that day? What kind of horrible adventure would I have gone on from there? What would my ending have been?

Recovery has been a long road—longer than I thought it would be—and often harder to accept than I anticipated. During the first year of recovery, I hated to look at my body. Sometimes I'd glance in the mirror with disgust, cursing the new thickness that layered the bottoms of my upper arms, pinching it between my fingers as if measuring my defeat. Other times I'd catch myself mindlessly cradling my lower stomach with my right hand, instinctively covering it so no one would see it, so no one would comment on how much weight I'd gained or tell me how much better I look now. Sometimes when people would say, "You look so healthy," I wanted to punch a wall instead of saying thank you.

Those feelings come rarely now, and when they do, they flash, because I won't let them stay. I talk myself through them until those toxic thoughts leave, so I can continue on with this beautiful new life where I can finally eat, where I feed my body like a human body is meant to be fed, and where I love myself the way I always should have, the way I never knew how to before.

I'm still in therapy twice a week with Ilene and Theresa. I still get scared of new foods sometimes, and I still have moments of guilt after I eat. I was addicted to being thin, and as with any addiction, a piece of it will lie dormant in me forever. Anorexia was my drug, and feelings of starvation flowed through my veins like heroin, making me feel powerful and unique. Being skinny made me feel things that weren't real, a false sense of acceptance, the illusion of glamour and worthiness. I'm not foolish enough to believe that the bridge leading back to the other side has crumbled, but I'm strong enough now to put every barrier in the way of crossing over ever again.

I am firmly on the other side, and I will never go back. My husband is here. My children are here.

I never thought I could recover, but I knew life would change if I could find a way there. I knew my health would improve, and it has. My resting heart rate has come up drastically. My blood pressure is normal. My liver inflammation has dissipated. My bones are stronger, my hair is thicker, my skin is clearer. I knew all that could happen, and I'm intensely grateful that my body waited for me to find my way back to health.

But I didn't anticipate the rest of the changes. There was a world of gifts waiting for me on this side.

There used to be a chill that would sit in my bones, a biting pain that formed an unstoppable shiver when my body got cold. Now I walk through spring days in short sleeves without blistering pain from the wind. I'm outside with my children on winter days, and the cold stays on my skin instead of seeping inside me and shaking me from within. I can sit in air-conditioning without my body feeling tortured. That is my life without anorexia.

I used to plan my meals in advance, everywhere I went, writing my meal plan on paper and checking it over and over for accuracy. I hardly tasted the food I ate, my focus almost entirely on the parameters of what I was entitled to eat, on obeying the rules on the papers that were always in my bag. That's finished, the papers long gone and the rules in my past. I can walk into any restaurant and open a menu for the first time, and there's always something I want. My eyes scan the pages for what my body is in the mood for, and while I eat, I can focus on everything around me, the tastes, the smells, the people. Restaurants are exciting, and eating gives me joy. That is my life without anorexia.

I used to exercise through anything. I sprinted through tendinitis, soaked my surgical bandages in sweat, fought for breath between coughs as my Covid-ravaged body pushed the pedals on a stationary bike for hours. I am free from that now. My exercise is slower, I don't fight for breath, I don't allow myself to be in pain. I take days off, I let my body recover, I run slower. Sometimes instead of jogging, I try new things that I've always wanted to try, like boxing and tennis. When I'm sick, I lie on the couch and rest, like I always dreamed I'd be able to do one day. That is my life without anorexia.

I used to think compulsively about food and weight every minute, every day. Once my mind was freed from those compulsive thoughts, I had room once again to think about other things. There was space to wonder about new career ventures, new friendships, decluttering my home, writing a book. That is my life without anorexia.

I take long trips with my family without worrying about the meals.

I eat ice cream with my children. I don't drown in guilt afterward.

In the late summer of 2022, I had dinner with friends at a bustling New Jersey steak house where the portions arrive piled high on fancy plates and white tablecloths are covered in steaming masses of food. It was the kind of place that had always scared the life out of me. I wasn't worried that night; I was comfortable with restaurants by then, and my eating had stabilized. But I hadn't yet come to terms with the weight I'd gained.

I felt bad about my body, especially that night, which was somewhat understandable, considering the company. Of the two couples we were meeting, both wives were now thinner than I was, something I was getting used to after a lifetime of being the skinniest woman in almost every room I'd walk into. I looked at their bodies. Their skin didn't puff out under the straps of their tank tops next to their breasts, as I had watched mine do when I'd gotten dressed that night, pressing the puffs with my pointer finger to see if I could stuff them away. Their stomachs didn't roll on top of their pants when they sat down, the way mine was doing as I sat there trying not to hate my body. The men sat at one end of the long table and the women sat at the other, and despite my silent preoccupation, the mood was festive as we talked about life, our kids and plans for the fall. The conversation then turned to my health.

"How are you doing with recovery?" my friend asked. "Food-wise, I'm great," I said. "I'm eating everything, and I feel healthy. I'm just still learning to accept the weight gain."

"How much weight do you think you've gained?" my other friend asked. I told her I hadn't stepped on a scale since before I started therapy, in over a year. "If I had to guess, I'd say maybe twelve to fifteen pounds. But I really have no idea," I said. One of the husbands turned his head to join the conversation. "You look great," he said to me. "You don't need to weigh yourself, you can probably just guess. I think you look about one-forty now."

"I'm not one-forty," I shot back, my heart pounding. "I'm not one-forty," I said again, looking at my friends, frantic to convince them—and myself—that I hadn't gained that much weight. One-forty meant I was getting bigger too fast, that I was out of control, that I was nearly the same size as when I met Evan. Suddenly, the food looked disgusting to me, and I didn't want any of it. "You don't look one-forty," said my girlfriends. "That's ridiculous, don't listen to him. Men have no idea," they insisted. But 140 was all I could think about the rest of the night, and the next day, and the day after that. *I look one-forty. I'm back to one-forty.*

In the days and weeks following that dinner, I thought a lot about that number and how much power it had over me. That number had enough power to ruin my night, to fill my mind with negative thoughts, and to consume me with worry. It was a number, and it wasn't even real, it was just one man's drunken opinion. It was one person pulling digits out of the air. It was meaningless, but it had been powerful enough to take all of my peace.

Learning to eat was only part of the battle; it was only a fragment of true recovery. Learning to accept myself, regardless of what the world thought of me, was the other part. Once I realized that, true recovery began. I finally understood that I'd never get past my eating disorder until I stopped looking for validation from the outside, in other people's opinions of my body, in the flashing numbers on a scale, in a stupid tag that hung on the inside of my pants. All of it was meaningless. All of it kept anorexia there in waiting, in case I needed it again.

It took me forty-six years to love myself unconditionally and to understand that true freedom is not caring about what other people think of you. That happiness can't be added up and measured in a notebook. That you can't run your way toward acceptance. That skin and bones don't make you special. It took me a lifetime to realize that beauty has no weight.

There is no weight of beautiful.

There is just me.

AUTHOR'S NOTE

There are many resources available to support the understanding of and education about eating disorders. One of those resources is the National Eating Disorder Association, www.nationaleating disorders.org. However, the mention of specific treatments or organizations in this book does not imply endorsement by the author or publisher. Readers should consult with their own medical, health, or other professionals before adopting any of the suggestions in this book or drawing inferences from it.

ACKNOWLEDGMENTS

I'd always dreamed about writing a book, but I never imagined it would be this one, a book filled with my deepest secrets about an illness I tried to hide from everyone, including myself. This book wouldn't exist without the love and encouragement of the incredible people in my life.

To my husband, Evan, who has stood by me in sickness and in health, I love you endlessly. Thank you for being my rock, for wiping my tears, and for always telling me I'm beautiful. I can't wait to finally travel the world with you.

To my children: Jonas, Adin, Hudson, and Alexis, you give me a million reasons to want to live forever. Being your mother has been my greatest joy. I'll always be sorry for the experiences I missed out on when you were little, but I promise to spend the rest of my life sharing ice cream with you. I love each of you so much.

To my parents, Ann and Barry, thank you for everything you sacrificed to give me this beautiful life, for encouraging my success, and for always cheering me on. I love you both.

To my brother, Eric, you are the happiest person I've ever known, and your happiness is infectious. You've taught me empathy and kindness, and how to forgive and forget. Thank you for being my best friend, the best brother, and for letting me tell your story with mine.

To my grandparents, even though you're no longer here, you continue to inspire me. I miss all of you every day, and your stories still touch my life.

To my castmates, the ones who have become like family, thank you for making this wild ride so fun, and for always picking me up when I fall. I know we'll be friends for life.

To Ali, Cindy, Hannah, and the Tenafly mommies who've been the best friends I could ask for, thank you for your endless support and encouragement, and for being my greatest cheerleaders. I adore each of you.

To Francis Berwick, Noah Samton, Pamela Gimenez, and all of the incredible people I've worked with at NBC/Universal, thank you for having faith in me, and for giving me the platform to share my story. I mean it when I say this show saved my life, and I'll forever be grateful.

To Andy Cohen, thank you for letting me recover so visibly, and for handling my story with such compassion. I love being a part of the Bravo family.

To Courtney Paganelli, my fabulous literary agent, thank you for wanting my story, for loving my writing, and for your constant reassurances. This book wouldn't exist without you.

To my magnificent editor at Simon & Schuster, Natasha Simons, thank you for your skillful insight, for bringing this book to life, and for making my author dreams come true.

To my brilliant team at Gallery Books, Jen Bergstrom, Aimee Bell, Sally Marvin, Lauren Carr, Bianca Ducasse, Caroline Pallotta,

Mia Robertson, and everyone else who helped shape this book, I couldn't imagine working on this with a better group of people. Thank you for your time and your wisdom.

To my cover shoot team, the supremely talented John Vairo and Chad Griffith, and my gifted glam squad Jamal Tadros and Karlene Damallie, every time I look at the cover of the book I am blown away. It's gorgeous, perfect, and exactly what I hoped it would be.

To my PR gurus, Tom Ierna and Anthony Lario, you guys are simply the best. Thank you for all your hard work since day one.

To Ilene Fishman, my incredible therapist, what a ride this has been. Thank you for letting the cameras into our sessions, and for working so hard to help me live without an eating disorder. I am not the same woman who walked into your office in 2021; I am a thousand times stronger and healthier, and I owe so much of that to you.

To Theresa Kinsella, my extraordinary dietician, thank you for answering every silly question I've asked, for helping me love food again, and for never giving up on me. We have some work left to do, but I promise to cross the finish line one day.

To Elissa Altman, my writing teacher, thank you for making me feel like the most gifted writer you'd ever taught. The confidence you instilled let me write on another level and made this book as special as it is.

Last but not least, to fifteen-year-old Jackie, who dreamed that one day she'd be good enough to be picked up on someone's pinkie. You were always good enough. You were always beautiful. I love you.